Toddler's tantrums

Alison Mackonochie

...lished in 2006 in the United Kingdom by

& Brown Publishers Limited
20 Lonsdale Road
London NW6 6RD

Editor Tom Broder
Designer Anne Fisher
Photography Jules Selmes

Text © 2004, 2006 Alison Mackonochie
Illustrations and compilation © 2004, 2006 Carroll & Brown Limited

A CIP catalogue record for this book is available from the British Library

ISBN 10: 1-904760-40-6
ISBN 13: 978-1-904760-40-5

The moral right of Alison Mackonochie to be identified as the author of this work has been
asserted in accordance with the Copyright, Designs and Patents Act of 1988

Reproduced by Colourscan, Singapore
Printed and bound in Barcelona by Bookprint

Note The information contained in this book is not intended as a substitute for
professional medical advice and diagnosis. While the advice and information are believed
to be accurate at the time of going to press, neither author nor publisher can accept any
legal responsibility or liability for errors or omissions.

contents

foreword

Not for nothing is the period between the ages of two and three years commonly known as the "terrible twos". This is the age when most toddlers start testing the boundaries set by their parents to find out just how much they can get away with. The desire to feel safe and babied starts to conflict with a desire to be more "grown up". Add to this the frustration of wanting to do things that are physically beyond their capabilities and it is easy to see why children often find this stage of development difficult. It's not easy for parents either, which is why adults and toddlers can often find themselves on a collision course.

An awareness of how your child is feeling and the reasons behind his actions will help you cope with bad behavior and tantrums. This book is a complete guide to the parenting skills needed to get through this stage. It discusses the different types of bad behavior and suggests the best way to handle your child. It covers the situations that often cause tantrums and explains how to steer clear of confrontation. And, because it isn't always possible to avoid problems, it outlines the most successful strategies for dealing with your toddler's outbursts.

Children are not born naughty and difficult, although this may be hard to believe when faced with your toddler's anger and frustration. These are traits that develop as your toddler struggles toward independence. With your help, your toddler can come through this "difficult" phase and grow into a secure and loving child.

1 Parenting skills

All toddlers misbehave – some occasionally, some much more frequently. You may not know exactly when your child's next outburst will occur, but you do have control over how you choose to deal with it. Having the right parenting skills will make it much easier to guide your toddler through this often difficult period of his development.

parenting styles

Children don't come with instructions or guidelines on how best to bring them up, so parents generally have to make up the rules as they go along. Your own parenting style is likely to be based on the way you were brought up, with the things that you liked about your mother's and father's style of parenting being used and the things you disliked discarded. You also can learn a lot from watching and talking to other parents, listening to their advice and deciding what will work for you.

Much of what you do will be based on trial and error, with some techniques working well for your child while others do not. Your first child is usually the "guinea pig" and you are likely to try out a variety of different ideas before settling on the ones that work best for you. This will produce some tried and tested ideas on parenting, but it is important to remember that every child is unique and you may need to change your methods to suit a new sibling.

Your child's temperament

If you and your child have similar characters you will find it much easier to empathize with your child and understand his behavior. If your

No two children are exactly the same and you may need to adapt your parenting methods to suit different temperaments. Try to treat your children as individuals.

temperaments are very different, you will have a much harder time identifying with him or understanding why he misbehaves. Most experts believe that a child's basic temperament is there at birth and is reflected as he grows in the way he approaches, interacts in and experiences social relationships. However, research also suggests that traits can change as a child develops and can be modified by different parenting styles and environmental factors.

Nature or nurture?

This balance between the inborn "nature" and the subsequent "nurture" of a child has been the subject of many studies into children's temperament and behavior over the past 50 years. In the 1950s, the prevailing view held that nurture accounted for most of the differences in temperament among children – if a child had behavioral problems his parents were usually blamed. This approach, however, could not explain why children respond differently to the same parenting methods.

The opposing view held that temperament was due to largely hereditary or inborn influences. But many studies have shown parents to have a far greater influence on behavior than this theory seems to allow. In the light of this, researchers have suggested that nature and nurture are a part of the same picture, with both contributing to the development of temperament. Today, most people feel that children are born with certain "natures," but parents provide the "nurture" and can help change negative aspects of behavior.

Your own temperament

Parenting is a two-way process, and the way you react to your child's behavior depends largely on your own temperament. Someone with a calm, easy-going nature is likely to be less stressed by bad behavior than someone who gets uptight and easily anxious. You may have strong ideas about how a child should behave and if your child doesn't fit into this pattern you may well feel disappointed, even angry with him.

Sometimes, it may happen that you and your child's natures are so different you can't help but rub each other up the wrong way. If this is the case you'll need to take control of the situation. In extreme cases, you may need to work through the differences with a professional who will be able to help you find ways of dealing with them. The important thing is to remember that once differences have been identified it is easier to avoid problems before they get out of hand. See page 8 for advice on managing your emotions.

Finding the right style

Although it can be hard, you need to remember that your child is an individual in his own right and with his own temperament – he is not an extension of you, so you cannot reasonably expect him to behave as you would. You can certainly try to guide your toddler's development and instill positive qualities, but try not to have too many preconceptions about what he should be like or how he should act.

Instead of trying to change your toddler's temperament, look for and encourage his natural talents and abilities. Your child does need some form of structure and discipline in his life, but he also requires love, support and understanding if he is to flourish. You can invest a lot of time and energy in trying to change your child, but often the best you can do is simply provide him with the guidance and support he needs to thrive.

coping with your emotions

There is no doubt about it, some toddlers seem almost programed to drive their parents to distraction. Easy-to-manage children are generally easy to like, but a toddler with a strong will who constantly tests his boundaries can be much harder to feel positive about. If yours is one of these, don't feel bad about the way he makes you feel – it's quite natural to experience anger and frustration when your child is pushing you to the limit of your tolerance.

It's not a bad thing for your child to know that you are angry, but try not to lose control and make sure he understands *why* you are angry. Try telling him "I am feeling angry about the broken vase," rather than "I'm angry with you for breaking the vase." This way, you are conveying your emotions to your child without making him feel inadequate or belittled.

Taking time out

There may be times when you feel at your wits' end and are tempted to lash out verbally or even physically. Neither of these actions will achieve anything constructive. You will simply frighten your child or, in some cases, make him feel that his behavior has obtained exactly what he wanted from you – your attention.

If you do feel yourself losing control, you may find it helps to put some space between you and your child. It might be easiest to remove yourself from the scene – once you've explained to your child why you are walking away – or you may prefer to give your child some "time out" (see page 70). Make sure that he understands that you are going to calm down and will be back soon, and make sure he is safe while you are apart.

Sharing the load

Looking after a disruptive toddler can be very tiring, so try to create some time for yourself. You are much more likely to have trouble controlling negative emotions if you are feeling run down or exhausted. Don't try to be a martyr – if you are having problems coping ask for more help from your partner, get friends or relatives to lend a hand or ask your doctor for advice on support services.

Keeping things in perspective

It is easy to get so involved in the day-to-day business of toddler rearing that you lose sight of the wider picture. When you are next feeling particularly upset or resentful of your toddler's behavior, take a moment to stop and remember exactly why you love him.

BECKY NEEDED RULES

When Becky reached the 'terrible twos,' Bob and I couldn't agree how to handle her behavior. We really fell out over this, which put a terrible strain on our relationship. Becky picked up on these feelings and constantly played us off against each other. It wasn't until we agreed on some house rules and stuck to them that we were able to address Becky's behavioral problems.

An emotionally demanding toddler can easily distract attention from quieter siblings. Find the time to give everyone a bit of one-to-one attention and try to avoid making any positive or negative comparisons.

The effect on the family

A badly behaved or strong-willed child can have a devastating effect on the family if allowed to do so. The stress of constantly coping with bad behavior can leave you feeling exhausted and short-tempered and may cause rows between you and your partner. Other siblings may be affected – a quieter, more passive child is easily overlooked when a more demanding youngster monopolizes the attention. Alternatively, favoritism may occur because the easier child is so much nicer to be with, leaving the troublemaker feeling left out and unloved.

In this type of scenario you will need to work hard to keep the family on an even keel. Talk to your partner about the best way to handle difficult situations and agree some principles that you both will stick to. Work as a team and try to back each other up, even if you don't always agree on the best way to approach the situation. Focus on a few important rules and let your children know these are non-negotiable. Once everyone understands that you and your partner are together on this, there is less incentive to beg, plead or cause a fuss, and less temptation to try to play you off against each other.

avoiding power struggles

Your toddler has an amazing amount of power over you and he may exert this any time he doesn't get what he thinks he wants or needs. He has only limited self-control at this age, but he is very good at using this lack of control to get his own way – he acts on whim, has little

Toddlers are very good at exploiting maternal instincts to get their own way. Try to recognize the difference between a genuine request for attention and an attempt to emotionally bully you.

appreciation of the rights of others and is perfectly prepared to shout, whine and scream to get what he wants.

Faced with this armory of psychological weapons, it is little wonder that parents often feel it is easier to give in to their toddlers' demands than to stick to any rules. But while it is good for your child to learn he has some influence over those he loves, it is important not to let him bully you or wear you down.

Testing your boundaries

A child who has a mind of his own will test you far more than one who is more easy-going. This is because he needs to experience the boundaries that you set repeatedly before he will accept them. If your boundaries are unclear or ineffective, you can expect problems because your child will simply push past them to see how far he can go. Strong-willed children bring out strong reactions, so don't be surprised if your child makes you feel exhausted or overwhelmed.

Maintaining your authority

Toddlers are very good at power games, mainly because they get a lot of practice. As your child grows and develops he will quite naturally start to challenge your authority and push at the boundaries you have tried to put in place. This is perfectly normal and is vital to your toddler's developing independence – but it has to happen in an acceptable way and it has to have limits.

If you are constantly having power struggles, you may need to examine the methods you use to discipline and control him to see how effective they are. If they lack clarity and firmness they

The world can be a very confusing place for a young toddler. If you listen to his concerns and talk to him about his feelings he is less likely to seek an outlet for his frustrations in bad behavior.

Signs of a strong will

If your child fits any of these descriptions he is likely to be stubborn and single minded. You need to set very clear and consistent boundaries:

☑ He refuses to do things he doesn't want to do

☑ He demands constant attention

☑ He argues every point

☑ He has frequent temper tantrums

☑ He pushes things to the extreme

☑ He is aggressive

☑ He turns everything into a fight or a struggle

☑ He wants to do everything for himself

could actually be encouraging the behavior you are trying to stop. Your toddler will be much happier knowing there are boundaries.

Power sharing

While your child does need to recognize that he can't always get his own way, you don't want him to feel he has no influence over you and no outlet for his frustrations other than bad behavior. Try to show him that asking nicely for things is much more likely to get him what he wants than throwing a tantrum. Include him in decisions that affect him so that he can have his say. Even if you decide not to allow your child to have what he wants, your child will know that the adults in his world have not simply dismissed his request.

Listening and talking to your child is very important. He will learn from everything you say, so if you discuss his feelings with him it will help him to realize that it is all right to feel the way he does, whether this is angry, miserable or content. You will be able to explain that it is how he manages these feelings that is important.

positive parenting

Your child depends on you to provide the emotional support that he needs to get through toddlerhood. If he learns from you that he is a unique and valuable person, he will take this with him into adulthood. Children who are not given this belief in themselves often spend their lives looking for love and acceptance – and may express these insecurities by behaving badly.

Much of your toddler's behavior is driven by his need to understand himself. His self-image is a reflection of what the people around him say to him, so if you tell your toddler he is "a good boy" or "very naughty" that is how he will perceive himself at that moment. Constantly criticizing your toddler for bad behavior can reinforce a negative view of himself, which may well be counter-productive to good conduct.

Self-esteem

Try not to use sarcasm or unkind words when you talk to your toddler. He will believe what you tell him, so informing him crossly that he is "very bad" or "the naughtiest boy in the world" will knock his self-esteem. Of course there will be times when you need to reprimand him – if he hurts another child, for example – but you should avoid labeling him. Tell him that what he has done is bad, not that *he* is bad. It's vital to give him confidence in himself and to build his self-esteem, not undermine it.

Love and attention

Giving your child unconditional love and acceptance is one of the most important things you can do as a parent. This doesn't mean you should be blind to your toddler's faults or that

Building self-esteem

✓ Tell your toddler frequently how much you love him

✓ Demonstrate your affection with lots of hugs and kisses

✓ Let him know that he's wonderful and that you enjoy being with him

✓ Listen to what he has to say so that he knows you find him interesting and enjoy listening to him

✓ Give praise for effort and attempting to do things, as well as for succeeding, and show him that it is fine to make mistakes

✓ Encourage your toddler to try things on his own and give him the opportunity to make some of his own decisions

you should condone bad behavior, it just means that whatever he does and however he behaves he knows that you will continue to love him. He needs to understand that you love him for who he is, not what he does.

Getting this message across to your toddler may not be as easy as you first think. Your toddler is likely to believe that when you are cross you don't love him anymore. He is not a mind reader. He won't know that when you are angry with him this doesn't in any way affect your love for him.

Showing your love

The simplest way to let your toddler know how you feel about him is to tell him. But more than this, you also need to show him how much you care. The more you let him know that you love him through your words and actions, the more likely he is to grow up to be happy, secure, self-confident and well-adjusted.

One of the most important ways of doing this is by giving him lots of attention. If your toddler doesn't get the attention he needs from you he may feel that he doesn't deserve it, so no matter how many times you say, "I love you" the statement will mean no more to him than words.

The other important part of this unconditional love is physical contact – there is nothing like a warm, loving hug to reinforce your words and actions. Even when your toddler has been particularly awful and you are feeling very fed up, try to find it within yourself to hold out your arms and give him a cuddle. A hug lets your child know that even though you are cross, you still love him and understand how hard this growing-up business can be.

Validating your child's emotions

Even the best-natured child sometimes feels emotions such as jealousy, anger and frustration. To a toddler, this type of feeling can be very confusing and upsetting. You need to show your child that these emotions are perfectly normal and acceptable – it is how he deals with them that is important. Let him know you empathize with him and understand how he feels, but explain that he needs to find a socially acceptable way to express his frustrations.

Encouraging individuality

Every child is unique, so the skills you need to be a parent to your child are unique too. What works for one parent may not work for another and it's important not to get drawn into a competitive world where children and parents alike are compared and found wanting Hard as it may be, you should avoid comparing your toddler to other children or trying to make him into something he's not. If your toddler has a physically active temperament he is unlikely to sit

Words aren't always enough to show your toddler how much you love her. If you show her how much you care – by being with her and showing interest in everything she does – your words will have much greater meaning.

still long enough to show much interest in learning letters and numbers; if he has a quiet disposition, you shouldn't expect him to be first out onto the soccer field.

Accepting your child the way he is and being the best parent you can be is all that anyone can reasonably expect – and, more importantly, all you can expect of yourself. Have confidence in your parenting skills and don't allow others to undermine your belief in yourself. There is no right way to raise children so long as you give them what they need to feel happy and secure.

Positive feedback

You can help your child learn good behavior by highlighting the good things he does rather than always pointing out the bad. Praise and encouragement are sometimes all a child needs to learn how to behave. The difficult part for parents can be finding something to praise rather than criticize. It is all too easy to notice bad behavior and to take good behavior for granted. By focusing on the positive rather than the negative you can reinforce good conduct and improve your child's self-esteem. Of course, there will still be times when you need to tell your child that he's done something wrong, but you should avoid the temptation to constantly find fault with his behavior.

If you do need to say something, criticize the behavior rather than your child and try to offer some constructive guidance on how he can behave better. Above all, let your toddler know that it is perfectly acceptable to make mistakes – they are a vital part of his learning process.

Finding things to praise

To use positive feedback to improve behavior you need to find the opposite to the bad behavior and praise it. If your child frequently fights with his younger brother, wait until he is playing nicely with his brother and tell him how proud you are of him for not fighting. Over time, your child will come to realize

Remember to praise your child for good behavior – for playing quietly or for being helpful – rather than simply focusing on the times she's naughty.

Give your toddler the support he needs to attempt new challenges and develop new skills. Provide plenty of encouragement but make sure he knows that it is fine to make mistakes.

that it's much better to be praised for playing nicely than it is to be scolded for fighting.

Using this form of positive feedback will help build your toddler's self-esteem and encourage him to become more self-motivated. Praising your child for what he has done right will teach him to value himself: you are not just teaching him to obey you for the sake of avoiding punishment, you are teaching him control of himself for him own happiness and wellbeing. This type of approach will also help you, as a parent, to fully appreciate all of your toddler's more positive qualities.

What your child needs

Help your child feel happy and secure by providing him with all of the following:

✓ **Love** Making him feel wanted and valued

✓ **Consistency** Knowing what the limits are gives him security

✓ **Self-esteem** Helping him to develop a sense of self-worth

✓ **Praise and encouragement** Giving him the courage to go on developing

✓ **Attention** Showing an interest in him and everything he does

setting limits

Your toddler needs a structured, organized environment if he is to feel happy and secure. He likes to know when to expect mealtimes and bedtime, when it is time for his bath or when to go to playgroup. On top of these practical things, he needs to know the behavioral limits that will be tolerated by you and by others. This doesn't mean you should dictate exactly what your child has to do in a given situation – he should learn to make his own decisions. But he does need to know how far is too far. Once you have decided on these limits, be consistent and stick to them, no matter how much your toddler tries to push the boundaries.

Try not to fall into the trap of repeating, "how many times do I have to tell you?" Having to repeat this could mean that you didn't explain the limits calmly and clearly enough the first

"COUNTING TO TEN

Sara really knew how to wind me up – I'd try to remain calm, but sometimes she made me so angry I wanted to scream at her. Instead, I'd take a deep breath and count to ten very slowly, ignoring her completely while I did it. This gave me a chance to calm down before dealing with the situation. It didn't improve Sara's behavior but it certainly helped mine!"

Encourage your family and friends to back you up and stick to the house rules when they are looking after your toddler.

time. Above all, don't give in to your child's bad behavior or tantrums – if you do, you will have started something that will be very difficult to stop. If your toddler has managed to make you give in to something he wants once, he will certainly try hard to make you give in again.

Your behavior

You need to be in control of yourself and the situation, and your toddler needs to know this. If you blow your top at his behavior he will think *you* are having a tantrum. This may frighten him – he wants to know that you are in control. Of course, there may be times when you just aren't

able to help yourself and you lose your temper. After this has happened you will need to apologize to your child and give him a hug. Your toddler needs to know that you always love him, no matter how badly he has behaved.

Being consistent

Your toddler has expectations that he will test out on you. He will expect you to say "no" to dangerous things like touching the fire, but he will still ask whether he can do it. Equally, he will expect you to say "yes" when he wants to do something helpful like help to set the table. These areas are straightforward for a growing child because they can work out what to expect.

It's the areas where "no" may sometimes be "yes," or *vice versa*, that cause the confusion. If your child asks if he can call granny on the phone, for example, you may sometimes say "yes" and other times "no." This makes it much harder for your child to know what to expect. The best thing you can do in these circumstances is to make your decision and stick to it.

If you change your mind as a result of his whining, crying and screaming your child will certainly use the same tactics again – in all sorts of circumstances. He will have learned that he has the power to make you behave in an inconsistent way. At times you may feel that you are continually repeating the same thing, but by being consistent your child should eventually respond to the boundaries you set.

Family and friends

Make sure that your family and friends understand your rules and ask them to be consistent too. Don't let people adopt the "just this once" routine – your child won't understand why you say no while someone else allows him to do whatever it is he wants. The rules also need to apply to others who come to your house,

---

Making the rules

There are many ways of setting limits. Here are a few suggestions for some of the things you should be thinking about:

- ☑ Set consistent rules about eating, bathing and bedtime

- ☑ Explain exactly why dangerous objects are out of bounds

- ☑ As far as possible, stick to routines so your toddler knows what to expect

- ☑ Have the same rules wherever you are – out visiting friends, in the park or in a shopping mall

- ☑ Put limits on the sort of behavior you find unacceptable

- ☑ Explain how any discipline you enforce works and be consistent

such as your child's friends. This may not make you very popular, but your toddler will be much more comfortable in the knowledge that he knows where everyone stands.

Public places

Being consistent isn't always easy and sometimes it would be a whole lot simpler and less embarrassing to give in, especially in a public place. But it is worth following through, even if it does leave you feeling red-faced. Your child needs to know that you mean what you say, whether you are at home or in public. If you give in once, your child will expect you to give in again – especially if he realizes that tantrums are more effective in front of strangers.

Shopping trips can leave everyone feeling tired and fractious and you may prefer to avoid a scene. But consistency is important, even if it risks embarrassment.

DAVID'S WARNING

David was misbehaving at a party so I told him to stop. When he didn't take any notice I warned him that if he carried on we'd go home. He continued to misbehave so I took him home. He cried and sobbed all the way there and I felt dreadful, but he hasn't misbehaved at a party since.

Threats and warnings

Threats are not punishments, they are an intention to punish. If you threaten your child with a punishment such as being sent to bed but don't enforce the threat when he repeats his bad behavior, the threat becomes meaningless. Your child will see it as a form of inconsistency and have no reason to believe you next time you threaten him. Sometimes you may carry out the threat, often after repeating it several times, but this only adds to your child's confusion.

If you warn your child that you will do something if he continues to behave in a certain way, you should always follow through if he repeats or continues his behavior. This way he learns you mean what you say. In some situations it may help to place a time limit on your warnings so that your child knows exactly how long he has to start or finish something before he is punished. This gives him time to prepare. You could even use an egg or oven timer to emphasize this time limit.

2 Types of bad behavior

Every toddler has her own particular pattern of behavior, and it's largely our interpretation of this behavior that defines whether it is "good" or "bad." Of course, there are some types of antisocial behavior that should be unacceptable under any circumstances – biting, hitting or hurting others, for example. But there are other sorts of behavior, such as whining, that you probably want to avoid. Before you can help your toddler overcome these tendencies you need to understand why she is acting in this way.

understanding your toddler

All toddlers test their parents by behaving badly, and they often pick a time and place where their behavior can have the maximum effect. One of the main reasons for this is to get your attention. Your child needs to know that she is the center of your world, and if she feels this isn't the case, she will find ways to grab your attention, even if it means annoying you or making you cross.

Your child's dependence on you can make her feel very insecure when your attention is withdrawn, even if only for a short while. This insecurity, often coupled with frustration because she can't verbalize how she feels, can lead to all sorts of antisocial behavior – as well as crying and screaming, she may hit, kick or bite you in an effort to get you to take notice of her.

For a young toddler, the world is a very bewildering and confusing place. She doesn't understand why she has to do things she doesn't want to do, and she may be frustrated by her inability to do the things that she does want to do. These frustrations can easily express themselves in bad behavior – especially since your toddler has only limited control over her impulses and little ability to predict the consequences of her actions. It's important to remember that very few toddlers do anything that is premeditated – most bad behavior is simply an immediate and impulsive reaction to a situation.

Toddlers can feel very insecure when they don't have your full attention. Sometimes, something as simple as talking on the phone or having a conversation with a friend can lead to an outburst.

On a bad day it can seem as though your child can find a hundred different reasons to misbehave, but in reality there are just a few main causes of bad behavior:

- Attention seeking – she wants your attention, even when it is negative

- Jealousy and competition – she doesn't like sharing

- Frustration – she physically can't achieve what she wants to do

- Separation anxiety – she hates being apart from you

- Reaction to illness, tiredness or emotional upset – she cannot explain how she is feeling and reacts badly

- Unrealistic expectations from adults – she's unable to achieve what is being asked of her

Realistic expectations

Understand your toddler's limitations and try to accept that you can't always expect her to behave in a completely mature or responsible manner. You need to suit your expectations to your toddler's mental, emotional and physical phase of development. Just as you can't expect her to stay dry if her bladder muscles are not yet physically capable, you shouldn't expect her to be happy to share a toy if she is not yet mature enough emotionally.

Demanding too much from your toddler will only leave her feeling anxious, insecure or confused. Don't expect more from her than she can realistically give. Encourage your toddler to aim high, but accept that she will sometimes make mistakes – when she does, forgive them.

Your child's development

It may come as a shock to see your delightful, amenable baby turn into a bad-tempered toddler, but it is important to realize that this change is a stage that all children go through. Some toddlers are naturally much more easy-going than others, but there is a great deal of common ground across this stage of development.

Your toddler is no longer a helpless baby who is dependent on you for everything – as she comes to realize that she's a separate human being, and that she doesn't have to do what you say or even stay where you put her, she will begin to test her boundaries. This may drive you mad, but it's a huge step forward in your toddler's development.

Behavior with other children

One of the hardest things to deal with is your child hitting, biting or being aggressive toward another child. Try to remember that a very young child doesn't understand that what she is doing hurts, so she has little or no concept of the other child's distress.

You can tell your toddler off and explain to her why her behavior is unacceptable, but you shouldn't expect a very young child to understand your reasoning. It isn't until around three years of age that she begins to have some understanding of how her actions can affect others. Before this she is more likely to be fascinated by the fuss that occurs when she hurts another child. She may even try it again just to see if she gets the same reaction.

whining ways

That awful voice that children use when they whine is guaranteed to drive parents mad. Whining when she wants something or she doesn't get her own way is the sort of behavior your child is likely to reserve for you, and those closest to her, where she knows it will have the maximum effect. Your four-year-old may whine about what she wears, what she will or won't eat, having a bath, going to bed – just about every part of her daily routine can become a battleground if you let it.

Whining is often accompanied by demands such as "I want," "let me," and "give me" – your child is testing out her new found individuality

and has worked out that, being the person she knows and trusts best, you are also the person most likely to give in to her demands. Older toddlers are usually worse whiners than younger ones because they are better able to express themselves as they try to assert their independence. This type of whining often peaks around the ages of four or five years – although the sooner your toddler realizes it won't get her what she wants, the sooner she is likely to stop.

How should you react?

Try giving your toddler a bit of space to be more grown up and avoid arguments about things that are not really important. If your child wants to eat apple pie for breakfast and cereal for tea does it really matter? Of course, you can't always give in to your child, but it will help if you sometimes let her have her own way.

You may be able to identify exactly what triggers a particular bout of whining – it won't necessarily be what your child seems to be demanding. Perhaps she is simply hungry, tired or bored. If you know what the trigger is you can respond appropriately. "I want" is often a signal for wanting attention, so a cuddle, a bit of praise or a few minutes spent doing something together may be all that is needed.

Your toddler may not even realize he is whining. Before you get angry with him for something he doesn't fully understand, make sure he knows how to recognize what he's doing. You could make a game out of it by covering your ears each time he starts to whine.

You may be able to divert a whiner by distracting her and getting her interested in something new. If this doesn't work, you must try to ignore her – or at least pretend to ignore her. Sometimes whining is impossible to ignore, and this is when the situation can get out of control. The more she whines, the more annoyed you become until you lose your cool. Before this happens, employ the "time out" technique (see page 70) to give both of you space to calm down.

Helping her understand

Something you should consider is the possibility that your child may not know that she is whining – she may not even understand what the word means. And, to be fair, it is very hard for her to stop doing something if she doesn't know what it is she is doing wrong.

Demonstrate to your child how she sounds by exaggerating the way she whines. Explain to her how much it upsets you and tell her that you can help her to stop doing it. Her curiosity is likely to get the better of her here and she'll want to know more. Suggest that every time you hear her making whining noises you will cover your ears or pull a face, and if she continues you will ignore her until she stops and talks properly. Ask her to decide which suggestion she prefers – she is more likely to go along with you if she has had some say in the remedy. At first this will seem like a fun game to your toddler, but if you stick to your side of the bargain she will quickly realize that whining is not the best way to get you to give in to her demands.

Giving praise

When your child uses her normal voice to ask for something, rather than her whiny one, don't forget to praise her by telling her how nice it is to hear her speaking like that. If you can, give her what she is asking for. If she wants a cookie

WATCH POINT...

IS YOUR CHILD UNWELL?

If your child is exceptionally or unusually whiney, always check for signs of illness. If whining is accompanied any of the following symptoms contact your doctor or other health professional for advice:

- A fever or temperature of 102°F (39°C) or above

- Intermittent vomiting over a six-hour period, or vomiting accompanied by fever and/or diarrhea

- Loose and watery stools that last for more than 48 hours, or stools with blood in them

- Pains such as a headache after a bump or abdominal pain

- Breathing difficulties, wheezing or chestiness

- Loss of appetite and lethargy over a 24-hour period

and you don't approve of giving cookies between meals, you could perhaps give her half a cookie, making sure that she knows why she is getting what she has asked for. This will help to reinforce the message that she is more likely to get what she wants if she asks you nicely.

the boredom factor

Very young children have short attention spans. They become bored very easily and may consequently revert to all kinds of antisocial behavior to get attention. An occasional period of boredom won't harm your toddler, indeed an over-stimulated child may benefit from the opportunity to learn how to entertain herself, but you should bear in mind that small children have a very limited capacity for independent play.

If you know your child is behaving badly because she's bored, the best way of dealing with this is to find some way of relieving her boredom or distracting her, although this can be quite trying if you have other things you should be getting on with. Where appropriate, try keeping her occupied with games or tasks that are similar to the type of thing you're doing yourself – if you have some paperwork to do, for example, you could give her some paper and crayons to play with.

Try to avoid using food as a cure for boredom. While there is nothing wrong with giving your toddler a healthy snack between mealtimes if she is hungry, using snacks simply to distract or bribe your child can risk encouraging an unhealthy attitude toward food.

Negotiation

Sometimes, the only way to deal with boredom is through negotiation. Try making a deal with your toddler – tell her that if she lets you finish

Try to involve your child in the household chores. This will stop her getting bored – and teach her to be more helpful round the house.

what you are doing you will take her for a walk, play a game or read a story. Allow her to choose the activity so that she feels she has some control over the situation. This works better with older toddlers. Children under two years have little concept of anticipation – their perception of life is focused on the "now." Your toddler should begin to grasp the concept of future reward between the ages of two and three.

Amusing your child at home

If you are trying to get the housework done, suggest your toddler "helps" you and make it into a kind of game by chatting to her about what she's doing. You will need to be prepared for the job to take longer than anticipated and for accidents to occur, such as spilt water during an attempt at washing up, but it should help keep her occupied. Try some of these simple chores:

- Show her how to rub polish into the tabletop and let her see how it shines when she's finished.
- Give her a bowl of water with some washing-up liquid and let her wash some plastic beakers or some cutlery that you're sure won't hurt her.
- Give her some pegs to play with when you hang out the washing.
- Let her help fold up clean washing and put items in the ironing basket.
- Give her a dustpan and brush so that she can help sweep the floor.

Distractions on the road

It isn't always possible for your child to join in with what you are doing. Car journeys are a very common source of boredom – the words "are we nearly there yet?" are enough to fill any parent with dread. But this type of boredom is understandable. Your child has no idea how long the journey is going to take and even if you tell her, her understanding of time is limited. She's strapped into a seat so she can't expend her

Let your child take some favorite toys with her on car trips, but don't rely on them to keep her occupied – you'll need a few songs or games to play too.

energy and you are busy concentrating on something other than her. From her point of view this is not much fun. Try some of these travel tips to make the journey less stressful:

- Make frequent stops so that your toddler can get out of the car and run around.
- Play story tapes or CDs.
- Play simple games like counting the number of blue cars you can see.
- Fix a toy bag to the seat in front of your child's and fill it full of things to amuse her.
- Sing nursery rhymes or songs together.
- Make sure that she is comfortable and not too hot, cold or hungry.

breaking the biting habit

Your toddler's milk teeth can make very effective weapons, and once she discovers this she is likely to use them with glee. Your child may have particular favorites who she has selected for teething practice – you, her brother or sister, or perhaps her best friend. On the other hand, she may not be fussy who she bites or which part of the body she sinks her teeth into.

Biting is usually the result of a passing impulse rather than a planned or malicious act. It may be done out of frustration or simply to protect something your toddler considers her own. Very often a toddler will start biting when she first goes to playgroup and will have grown out of this phase by the time she reaches the age of three.

If your child bites you or others occasionally you can take comfort from the fact that she is just going through a normal stage of development.

How should you react?

Your response to your child biting someone is likely to depend on the circumstances. If it is just an impulsive nip during a moment of excitement then a firm warning should be all that is needed. Remove your child from the scene immediately after it happens and say "No!" in a serious voice, with a stern expression. Very often, your toddler will be as scared of having bitten someone as the victim is at being bitten. If the biting is done in anger, as part of a temper tantrum, you also will need to deal with the tantrum (see chapter 5).

If your child bites another during a dispute, you could try encouraging her to comfort the upset victim, perhaps with a cuddle or by giving her the toy they were squabbling over. Only you can tell whether getting the biter and victim together is a good idea. Sometimes, it's better to allow the children space away from each other, but do this without labeling one as the aggressor and the other as the victim – both children need to understand that it was the action of biting that was bad, not the child.

Some experts believe that holding your toddler close for a short time after a biting incident can be effective. Young, active children don't like to be restrained, so if they are restrained every time

Biting is not usually a spiteful or premeditated act, but your child needs to understand that it's not an acceptable way to get what he wants.

If you can persuade toddlers to kiss and make up, they usually quickly forget to feel upset. If there is much ill-feeling, however, you may need to give both parties some space to calm down.

they bite, they usually decide quite quickly that biting is not such a good idea. Whatever you do, don't bite your child back. In the past, this practice was popular with parents, but it is now considered inappropriate. Children are encouraged to learn by example, but this sends out the wrong message.

To counter attention seeking

If your toddler bites when she wants to gain attention, you need to be careful not to give more of your attention to the biter than to the victim – a big telling off still puts the biter in the spotlight. After you have reprimanded your child, try ignoring her. Give the best toys and more of your time to the injured party.

Avoid constant talk about your child's biting. If she hears you discussing it with other parents, or if she is labeled with a negative nickname such as "little biter" or "Jaws," you may be unwittingly giving her the attention she craves. Excessive attention to this type of undesirable behavior can actually reinforce it.

If biting is persistent

If the biting is repeated, premeditated or is seriously causing pain and damage to the victim, stricter measures may be needed (see positive discipline, page 42). Biting that continues after the age of four may be as a result of other underlying issues that need to be addressed, and you may need to seek professional help.

Dealing with other parents

Biting is bad enough when it happens in your own home, but in front of other parents it can be extremely embarrassing. If your child is the biter, all you can do is remove her from the scene and reassure the other parents that you do not approve of her behavior. Explain that you will be keeping a closer eye on your child in the future.

If your child is the victim, you may be upset, but try to remain calm. One bite doesn't mean that the offence will be repeated, so don't ban the biter from your child's social life. Remain close to the children when they play again so you can intervene if neccessary.

> ## TOMMY'S BITING GAME
>
> When Tommy was a baby I treated his biting as a bit of fun. He'd bite me, I'd say 'oww,' and he'd laugh. Then, as he got more teeth and could bite harder, it really began to hurt. He still thought it was funny, but I didn't. Because it had been a game before, he found it hard to understand why I was getting angry with him. I really wish now I'd put a stop to it when he was younger.

aggressive behavior

It is quite normal for a toddler under the age of two to hit out, kick or push when she loses control of a situation – she reacts like this because it is the only way she knows how to deal with a situation that she finds difficult. The important thing is for you to remain in control when this happens. If you retaliate by hitting back or shouting, you will only frighten your child or reinforce her bad behavior.

Reasons for the behavior

Toddlers often use aggression to get their own way or to gain ownership of something that they want. This type of behavior is most common in children aged between two and three years. So long as your child doesn't learn she can get her own way by being aggressive, she should soon find other ways to achieve what she wants.

An older toddler who shows signs of aggression toward others is very often simply reacting this way because she feels overwhelmed. Your child is likely to be as upset by the situation she has created as you are, and if you overreact she may feel guilty and distressed. You will need to work with your toddler to help her learn control.

Children learn a lot from each other, so your child may have learned to hit out because she has seen other children do it, perhaps at playgroup or nursery, or has been victim of another child's aggression. Generally, this type of behavior is outgrown – if it continues until school age you may need to seek professional advice.

How should you react?

Try not to lose control in response to your child's behavior. So long as disputes are minor, keep your distance and let the children sort it out for themselves. If the situation develops into a fight you will need to intervene. Separate the children and keep them apart until they have calmed down. A very young toddler may need to be held until she is calm (see page 74).

Once she has calmed down, you will need to explain that hitting and other types of violent behavior are never acceptable. Tell her that you'll continue to stop her doing them until she learns to stop herself. Your child won't like feeling out of control either and she'll want to be able to stop herself. Gradually, over time, she should learn to overcome her aggressive feelings.

Talking about it

It's important to talk to an older child about feelings of anger or aggression. Do this after the event, when things have calmed down and you're on your own together. There is no point asking an angry child why she has just hit her friend, or pushed another child over – she'll be so caught up in her feelings she won't be able to tell you. Wait until you are on your own together and tell her that you understand why she was upset. Give her the time and space to use words to express herself. You may need to help her by suggesting how she could have handled the situation better.

Older toddlers may react well to a situation where they have to listen to each other. Sit one child down and get her to explain why she behaved the way she did, then ask the other toddler to say how she feels. Don't expect any great revelations – sometimes just the fact that they have faced up to the situation together is all that is needed to overcome the hostility.

Dealing with other parents

If your toddler is the aggressor, you will need to apologize and reassure the victim's parents that you won't tolerate this type of behavior. If she is the victim, you may want to suggest to the aggressor's parents that the children spend some time apart. Suggest they play together another day and that one of you keep an eye on them to prevent the situation happening again. Whatever tactic you use, don't be tempted to pretend the aggression hasn't happened. This behavior needs to be controlled or it can result in a child growing up to be a bully or being bullied.

Toddlers have limited social skills and often resort to aggression as the only way they can think of to get what they want. You will need to teach your child to handle the situation in a more socially acceptable way.

food refusal

Feeding a toddler can be fraught with problems and mealtimes can easily become a battleground. Parents have an in-built instinct to nourish their child, which can lead to feelings of failure if their attempts are rejected. Of course, your toddler is only concerned with how she feels that day.

Your child's appetite

Children have different tastes and appetites – some eat like birds, picking at everything that's put in front of them, some eat moderate amounts of foods without too much fuss and others wolf down everything on their plate, providing it is of their choosing.

Expect your toddler's appetite to fluctuate or almost disappear at times. She will go through phases that are affected by things such as growth spurts, her moods, even changes in the weather. She may get "stuck" on a certain food, refusing to eat anything else, and then without apparent reason reject it. It is easy to worry about this type of faddiness, but it doesn't necessarily mean your child is not getting the proper nutrition.

A balanced diet

Before you start worrying about deficiencies and malnutrition, work out what your toddler has eaten over the previous week. Studies show that toddlers usually eat a well-balanced diet over a period of time, even though they may only pick at certain foods on a given day. The box on the right shows the different food groups needed to provide a nutritious diet for your child – but there is no ideal amount for her to eat on any one day. If she is healthy and growing well there's probably not too much wrong with her intake.

Most toddlers go through a phase of refusing to eat or only eating certain foods. So long as your toddler enjoys a balanced diet over a period of time, a little fussiness is nothing to be too concerned about.

Persuading your child to eat

Don't overwhelm your child with large portions or too many choices – she may find them frightening. Instead, offer small amounts of a few different foods in a toddler-sized bowl or plate. Serving a variety of foods will help keep your child interested. Food needs to look appealing too, so spend a little time on presentation and making food fun. Supervise your child's liquid intake, as too much may kill her appetite.

Structure mealtimes so that your child knows what is expected of her – that you want her to eat when you eat, for example, or stay at the table until the meal is over. Don't expect her to sit still for more than 15 or 20 minutes, and don't force her to finish her meal if she really doesn't want to. Resist the temptation to offer alternatives such as candy or cookies. Don't use food as a reward or a bribe, or refuse to give it as a punishment, as this can encourage an unhealthy attitude toward food.

Children, like adults, have their own likes and dislikes when it comes to food, so it is quite possible that there are some foods your toddler will refuse just because she doesn't like them. It's also worth remembering that flavors and textures can affect your child – sometimes even switching brands can put her off a certain food. It may help to include her in the meal planning, starting with the trip around the store. If you give her a sense of control over what she eats she may be more enthusiastic about mealtimes.

A BALANCED DIET

PROTEIN This is found in meat, eggs and cheese, and plant sources such as beans and other legumes. Try to include one serving daily.

FAT Full-fat dairy products are a good source of fat. Include at least ½-pint (350-ml) full-fat milk a day, or two servings of cheese, fromage frais or yogurt.

CARBOHYDRATES These are found in bread, pasta, rice, corn, cereal or starchy vegetables such as potatoes. Aim to include at least one serving at each mealtime.

VITAMINS These are found in a variety of fruits and vegetables and are required in small quantities each day. Aim to give your toddler five servings a day. Fruit juice counts as one serving.

MINERALS Iron, zinc and calcium are important for your toddler's development. Iron is found in red meat, oily fish, fortified cereals, bread, eggs, dried fruits and legumes. Good sources of zinc include wholegrain cereals, meat and poultry, hard cheese, eggs and legumes. Calcium comes mainly from dairy foods.

WATER Your toddler needs to drink several glasses of water each day. Plain water is ideal, but you may like to flavor the water with a little fruit juice to make it seem more appetizing.

bathroom blues

Whether you are attempting to teach your toddler to use the toilet or simply trying to give her a wash, the bathroom can be the scene for all sorts of obstinate behavior.

Washing and bathing

Newborn babies are often frightened of having a bath, which is why it is a good idea to start with topping and tailing. Once they overcome their fear of water they usually enjoy splashing and playing in the bath. Sometimes, for no apparent reason, a toddler regains her earlier fears and refuses to go near the bath. If the sound of running water sends your child into a panic you may have to start all over again and reintroduce her to the bath gradually.

Taking it slowly

Begin by standing your toddler on the floor in the bathroom and sponging her down with warm water from the basin. Once she has accepted this, run a small amount of water into the bath and use this to sponge her down while she's still standing on the floor. Eventually, when she is feeling brave enough, encourage her to sit in the bath in an inch or two of water. Over a period of time, increase the amount of water. This whole process may take anything from a few days to a few weeks to complete.

During this time you need to be careful that you don't allow anything to frighten your child. Spluttering taps, gurgling plugs and slippery baths can all hold terrors for her. Place a non-slip mat in the bottom of the bath and encourage your toddler to play in the bath by introducing bath toys and lots of bubbles. If all else fails, join

Don't force your toddler to get in the bath if she seems frightened – take a step back and reintroduce the bath slowly. Once the fears have been overcome her bathtime will become the best playtime of the day.

her in the bath. Your toddler will feel a lot more confident if you are with her and you can both have fun bathing each other.

Toilet troubles

Potty training is another area that can become fraught with difficulties. Your toddler may simply refuse to cooperate or she may cooperate sometimes but still have frequent accidents. She may use her toilet habits as a means of controlling you and actually enjoy the fact that she has the power to make you cross – from her point of view, the more angry you get with her, the more control she has over your emotions.

Once potty trained, there is usually a reason if your toddler suddenly starts wetting or dirtying herself. This regression may be associated with the arrival of a new baby, a house move, illness or other upsets. Although it can be hard, you need to show your child understanding and not allow the situation to turn into a battleground.

When to start toilet training

One way to avoid toilet tantrums is to not start potty training before your child is both physically and emotionally ready. There's a wide age range during which a child is expected to master toilet training, with many experts suggesting that two-and-a-half years is the earliest you should begin. The box below suggests some signs to look out for to check whether your child is ready for potty training – make sure she has achieved at least some of these before you begin.

If your child has frequent accidents she is likely to be upset or embarrassed and becoming angry with her may make the situation worse. If you feel frustrated over mopping up for the tenth time that day, talk to your child about how you feel rather than yelling at her. Explain that you are feeling cross because all the cleaning up is making you tired and that it would be much better for both of you if she used the potty in future. By telling her how you feel and not fighting, you can prevent your child from using accidents as a way to get your attention.

Potty training

Your child should be ready for potty training when you can say yes to most of the following:

✔ She wants to come to the bathroom with you and understands what the toilet is for	✔ She is not worried about sitting on the potty or toilet
✔ She seems to recognize at least a few seconds ahead that she needs to go	✔ She is over the fascination of learning to walk and run and enjoys sitting to play
✔ She knows what it means to have a wet or dirty diaper and perhaps shows a preference to be clean and dry	✔ She expresses a desire to wear grown-up underwear and attempts to pull them up and down without help
✔ She says words that indicate that she wants to pee or poop	✔ She is in a willing, receptive mood rather than in a negative phase
✔ She stays dry for a few hours at a time and has regular bowel movements	✔ She can follow simple directions, such as those for washing her hands

bedroom battles

A toddler spends a great deal of time in her room, so it's no wonder it becomes the setting for some bad behavior. Bedtimes are notoriously difficult, but mornings can bring problems too.

Bedtime shenanigans

Many children protest about being sent to bed almost as a matter of principle. The problem is that the protest comes at the end of the day, when you are tired and may have a limited amount of patience left to deal with a difficult toddler. Sometimes, your child is overtired herself, so that anything that upsets her results in tears and tantrums. She may suffer from separation anxiety, be afraid of the dark or be worried about having bad dreams.

Even if your child does go to bed quietly, she may keep reappearing or calling for you to ask for drinks or for the toilet, or to complain that she has an ache or a pain. All this manages to delay the period when she has to go to sleep and keeps you on your toes.

How should you react?

Start by creating a regular bedtime routine that helps your child's mind and body relax before she gets into bed. Keep the time you've chosen as bedtime constant and avoid boisterous activities for at least half an hour beforehand. Get your child ready for bed, give her a bath, a cuddle and tuck her in. Read her a story or sing a lullaby, then say goodnight and leave as though you mean it. Don't keep going back into the room to answer requests for attention.

If your child gets out of bed, be firm and put her back without trying to reason with her. Each time she reappears, take her back to bed and don't get involved in conversations about what she wants – though you will need to check she's not unwell.

Your toddler may become tearful and upset when you put him to bed, but try to resist the urge to pick him up – he needs to learn that you mean what you say when you put him to bed.

This approach can be tough, but in the end you will both benefit as your child learns that bedtime is fixed and non-negotiable.

Night wakers can be treated in much the same way. Once you have established that your child isn't ill and have taken her to the bathroom if necessary, put her back to bed, tuck her in and firmly say good night. Night wakers can leave you exhausted, so you and your partner may need to take turns dealing with the situation.

Dressing difficulties

Mornings are another potentially problematic period. Your toddler may have some pretty strong views on what she will or will not wear, or she may resist you trying to dress her even when she has chosen her own clothes. Trouble may occur if your toddler decides she wants to do something for which she lacks the capability, for example, putting on her own socks and shoes. This results in frustration and anger, and if you are under pressure yourself – perhaps you're trying to get ready for work – this can lead to a full-blown tantrum.

Avoiding problems

The easiest way to deal with this issue is to try to foresee, and if possible avoid, difficulties. When you buy her clothes, look for garments that are easy for a toddler to put on. If choosing what to wear is a cause for argument, select the clothes the night before. Offer your child a choice, but don't make it too wide – select two items and ask her which one she wants to wear.

Allow plenty of time for your child to get dressed, even if this means you have to get up ten minutes earlier. By avoiding rushing her you are less likely to face resistance. Make dressing fun by chatting about the day ahead or asking your child to name the clothes or the colors she is wearing. This will also act as a distraction.

STAGES IN LEARNING

DRESSING

When it comes to getting dressed your child may be limited by her physical abilities. As she grows older, she should learn to master certain skills:

- **Two to three years** She shows an interest in dressing herself, but is more of a hindrance than a help

- **Three years** She can put on large items of clothing without assistance

- **Four years** She is able to do up large fastenings, such as dungaree buttons

- **Five years** She is now largely able to dress herself, apart from buckling her shoes

hyperactivity

This is a commonly used word to describe excessively active behavior. If your toddler is considered to be hyperactive this doesn't necessarily mean that she is suffering from the more extreme syndrome of Attention Deficit Hyperactivity Disorder (ADHD). She may simply be more active than other children, have a more impulsive temperament and need less sleep. Whether your child is hyperactive or not is to a large extent dependent on how she is perceived by you and others around her.

Surveys show that as many as 30 percent of parents describe their children as hyperactive during their pre-school years. This usually refers to a period of behavior that begins around the age of two, when a child becomes increasingly active and noisy. A hyperactive child's general behavior is similar to other toddler's, although amplified so it seems much worse – some doctors believe that hyperactivity is just one end of the "normal" spectrum of behavior.

Boys are far more frequently judged to be hyperactive than girls, possibly because they are generally more physically active and louder than girls.

Possible causes

There are many theories about the reasons for hyperactivity, but in most cases the exact cause is not known. It has been blamed on chemicals and other harmful substances in the environment, on food allergies and intolerances, and on artificial chemicals in food such as colorings, flavorings and preservatives. Links have also been made between hyperactivity and certain drugs, as well as caffeine, which is found in soft drinks and chocolate. There may be a genetic influence, since hyperactive tendencies often appear to be inherited. Rarely, it may result from minor brain damage to the child during pregnancy or birth.

A possible cure

There are almost as many theories about the treatment of hyperactivity as there are about its causes. One of the most popular is based on the belief that the major cause is intolerance to certain foods, so that the main treatment is to identify and eliminate these from your toddler's diet. Don't attempt this on your own – you should always consult a doctor before putting your child on any type of food-elimination diet.

The best-known diet for hyperactivity is the Feingold diet, named after a US doctor who promoted it for treatment of hyperactivity in the 1970s. This diet eliminates all foods containing artificial coloring, preservatives and salicylates – natural chemicals that occur in many fruits, including apples, bananas and oranges.

ADHD

Attention Deficit Hyperactivity Disorder (ADHD) is "true" hyperactivity – a pattern of restless, inattentive, impulsive behavior where your toddler can't sit still or pay attention for more than a few minutes at a time and has no concept of the results of her actions. Of course, all very young children have short attention spans

If your child displays the following signs for more than six months you should seek professional advice:

- He is easily distracted by his thoughts and surroundings

- He is unable to focus on any activity for longer than a few minutes

- He is over-active – unable to keep still or stop talking

- He acts impulsively, with no thought for the consequence of his actions

and often act impulsively, but this type of behavior usually improves as the child grows older. If your toddler's behavior doesn't improve over time and becomes more severe or persistent it may be due to ADHD.

Although the medical profession has recognized ADHD for some time, in the past it was often misdiagnosed. Children displaying the symptoms of ADHD were simply thought of as naughty and lazy, and in some cases their behavior was blamed on a low IQ. It was frequently suggested that bad parenting played a part in the condition and that children were simply being allowed to get away with disruptive behavior.

More recently, scientific studies using advanced neuro-imaging techniques have been carried out to show that the brains of children with ADHD are different from those of other children. These differences are thought to be genetic, occurring very early in life when the brain is developing. ADHD is a long-term, chronic condition – some children will grow out of it, but others will continue to suffer inattention and impulsive behavior into adulthood.

Other difficulties

If your child suffers from ADHD she is likely to have other problems such as difficulty in sleeping, a tendency towards aggressive behavior and possibly learning difficulties. Your toddler may also have a problem settling into playgroup, and have difficulty in forming relationships with others of her own age. ADHD is sometimes accompanied by developmental problems as such as dyspraxia (clumsiness) or speech delay.

THE **NATURAL** APPROACH

Sugary foods, especially those made with refined sugar, can cause a temporary surge in your toddler's blood glucose levels. Refined sugar also has little mineral content – particularly chromium, which your child needs to metabolize the sugar. The result is an excessive or inconsistent supply of energy, which can result in many of the symptoms of ADHD. Instead, offer your toddler snacks such as fresh or dried fruit, granola bars, and cakes or cookies made with unrefined flour.

How it's diagnosed

ADHD is difficult to diagnose because your child may show signs of having the condition but in reality just have a "difficult" temperament. Health professionals will look for symptoms that are severe enough to cause significant problems for your child and those around her.

They will also take into consideration your child's circumstances to make sure there is nothing happening at home that could cause the behavior, such as a divorce or other serious upset. They may also want to know how much opportunity your toddler has to enjoy physical activities during the day – many children become mentally over-stimulated but do not have the chance to get enough physical exercise to make them healthily tired.

Treatment

There is no one straightforward treatment for ADHD as healthcare professionals across the world are divided about the best course of action to take when dealing with the condition. The main medical treatment these days is through the use of drugs, and in some cases behavioral therapy may be used as well as or instead of medication. Other practitioners do not believe that medication is the best answer and advocate remedies such as diet, behavior modification or complementary therapies such as acupuncture, aromatherapy or reflexology.

What you can do

If you feel your toddler has ADHD you should see a doctor or other healthcare professional for diagnosis and advice. The important thing with ADHD, as with other behavioral problems, is to reassure your child that no matter how bad her behavior you will continue to love and be there for her. She needs to know that you can help her control the way she behaves, so you have to teach her that her feelings can be managed and expressed in ways other than bad behavior.

If you have a toddler with ADHD you are likely to be exhausted, so taking time out for yourself also is important. If the condition is causing difficulties within your family or affecting your relationship with your child you may find it helps to discuss your feelings with a family counselor.

3 Discipline

The aim of any form of discipline is to teach your child self-control so he can function happily and effectively in the world in which he lives. There is no blueprint that says what is and what isn't acceptable when it comes to disciplining your child and different parents take very different attitudes. The important thing to remember is that while discipline should be used to help your child learn to behave better, it should never be used to make him feel bad about himself.

approaches to discipline

To many people, the word discipline conjures up the idea of punishment or chastisement, but this doesn't need to be the case. The term is actually derived from the Latin word *disciple*, meaning "one who learns" – so the emphasis should be on teaching, rather than simply penalizing your toddler. Your ultimate aim should be to find a satisfactory method to teach and protect your child until he is old enough to take responsibility for his own actions and behavior. Punishment is simply one way – and not necessarily the most effective – for you to achieve this.

Another important goal of discipline is to teach your toddler right from wrong. If this concept is not introduced from an early age, it may be difficult for your child to properly appreciate it later, when it becomes important for him to understand the difference.

Some parents are naturally very permissive when it comes to discipline, others are far more strict. There are no right or wrong answers when it comes to choosing the approach you wish to take, but you should be aware of some of the potential effects.

Parental styles

Over the years a great deal of research has been carried out into the effects of different styles of parenting on children's behavior. Some studies have identified three basic approaches toward discipline taken by parents – authoritarian, permissive and authoritative – each one being governed by a distinct set of rules and priorities. In the end, the way you choose to discipline your toddler will depend largely on what you personally feel is reasonable and effective. But it helps to be aware of some of the advantages and disadvantages of these different approaches.

Authoritarian

Parents who adopt an authoritarian approach to parenting expect unquestioning obedience from their children. They usually have rigid views on behavior that are not open to discussion or negotiation. Even as toddlers, children are expected to be obedient and to show respect for their parents' authority.

Very often, authoritarian parents use physical or verbal punishment to enforce their will. Some studies suggest that this type of rigid regime can leave a child feeling incapable of asserting control over his own life. In turn, this can result in a child growing up to be withdrawn and fearful.

Permissive

This is the opposite approach to authoritarian parenting, but permissive should never be confused with indifferent parenting. Permissive parents set great store in showing their children unconditional love, and encourage them to express their feelings and their individuality freely. To this end, they place fewer limits on their behavior and attempt to guide them by reasoning rather than by enforcing rules.

It has been suggested, however, that this lack of structure can result in children developing little or no self-control and little desire to accept the consequences of their actions. They may appear immature for their age and their behavior may be demanding, inconsiderate or even aggressive.

JANE'S MEALTIMES

I wanted Jane to learn the importance of family mealtimes. As soon as she was old enough to sit with us, I tried to insist that she stayed at the table until the meal was over. Jane had other ideas and as soon as she had eaten enough she was off – nothing I said or did could make her stay at the table. In the end, I had to concede that my natural instincts as a parent were not suited to her age and temperament. She was simply too young to stay still for that length of time.

Authoritative

Parents who adopt an authoritative style – which falls somewhere in between the other two – take a more flexible approach. They set firm limits so their children know the rules, but also encourage discussion and a degree of independence. They are supportive and respectful of their children's needs and exercise control through reasoning with their children and explaining any rules or limits that need to be set.

Not surprisingly, studies suggest that children brought up in this way tend to be the most well-adjusted. They often grow up self-reliant, self-controlled and socially aware. Authoritative parenting allows parents to be firm and in control, but also warm and responsive.

Disciplinary techniques

The methods you use to discipline your child will be influenced by the way you were brought up, by your character, even by your lifestyle. You will also need to consider whether you and your partner can agree on a consistent approach to discipline – the old saying "together we conquer and divided we fall" certainly holds true when it comes to parenting. Whatever style of discipline you tend toward, it is important that to have realistic expectations of your toddler – the demands you make of him need to match his temperament and personality as well as his physical and emotional development.

Your ultimate aim should be to teach your child to discipline and control himself. Positive and consistent disciplinary techniques will help teach him about the consequences of his own actions, so that he learns to take responsibility for these actions for himself.

Positive discipline

Today, most experts and parents agree that an approach emphasizing the positive aspects of a child's behavior is usually much more desirable and effective than one based on punishment. Try to pay most of

your attention to your toddler's good behavior and turn a blind eye to insignificant annoying behavior or naughtiness. Reserve battles with your toddler for times when you have no choice – if your child is putting himself at risk, for example. Listen to your toddler, explain all your demands to him clearly, and try to set a positive example for him yourself.

Reasonable and simply explained limits are the key to this type of positive discipline. These rules give structure to your toddler's world and help him feel secure. They teach your child what is expected of him and show how he should behave. Don't go overboard – your toddler will quickly

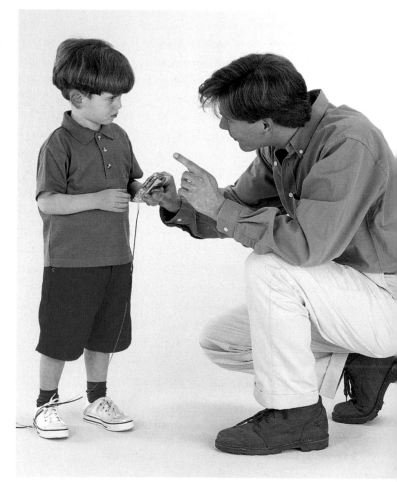

Your disciplinary techniques need to be appropriate to your toddler's age and understanding – if he is too young to realize that pulling the insides out of a tape means it won't work anymore, a simple reprimand may better than a punishment.

become confused by too many rules, or by rules that are not appropriate for his age, so limit the number you expect him to remember to a few age-appropriate, important ones. His language skills are still limited, so express any rules you make in simple terms that he can easily comprehend. This type of approach should make your toddler less inclined to present you with the sort of behavior that warrants punishment.

IGNORING BEN

Sometimes, at the end of a very long day, I deliberately choose to ignore Ben when he behaves badly. I know we are both tired and that any confrontation will simply result in us both becoming worked up and angry. I feel that under these circumstances ignoring him is the best course of action for both of us.

Punishment

There may, or course, be times when you feel that some form of punishment is both justified and necessary. Withholding an activity that your toddler enjoys – such as watching a favorite television program or being allowed to play with a friend – can help him learn that his bad behavior has consequences. As far as possible, though, it is probably best to reserve this type of discipline for times when your toddler seriously misbehaves. Punishment carries a negative message – it may teach him to avoid doing something bad, but it won't help him understand why other types of behavior are good. You want

your child to do something because he feels it is the right thing to do in that situation, not simply in order to avoid punishment.

Physical punishment, such as hitting or smacking, and some types of verbal punishment should be avoided. It's often hard not to shout at a naughty toddler, mainly because it is the easiest way to get his attention quickly. But, although this may have an immediate effect, it doesn't solve behavioral problems in the long term – indeed it often has a negative effect on behavior. The same applies to verbally threatening your child – although it is important to warn him about the consequences of overstepping the mark, you should never use these threats simply to bully or frighten him.

Making discipline easier

✓ Keep family rules to a minimum

✓ Use diversionary techniques rather than head-to-head confrontation

✓ Avoid situations that you know will trigger bad behavior

✓ Avoid battles over unimportant issues — concentrate on the ones that really matter

✓ Explain why certain behavior is wrong

✓ Respond to your child's bad behavior by withdrawing your attention

✓ Don't expect your child to be logical about his behavior

good communication

This is the key to solving most discipline problems – a lot of the fights and frustrations that occur between parent and child are the result of poor communication. Your attempts to discipline your toddler effectively will be much easier if he clearly understands your rules, appreciates the reasons behind them and knows that you will listen to him and take notice of his frustrations and grievances.

Your choice of words, your tone of voice, even your body language can make a big difference to the way your child reacts to your attempts to discipline him. An angry toddler may be so caught up in his emotions that he doesn't actually hear what you are saying, but he will still pick up on the way you are speaking, your expression and the way you hold yourself.

Just as important as the way you talk to your toddler is his ability to express himself to you. Your toddler learns to communicate effectively by observing you and other members of his family and listening to the way you all interact. Make sure your toddler is included in your family conversations. If he is left out, or if the conversation is too grown up for him to contribute to, he won't be encouraged to talk.

Talking to your toddler

When you are attempting to discipline your toddler it is particularly important to find the right tone. If you start your sentence with "you" and then continue with a criticism or complaint, your child will feel that you are making an attack and will immediately be on the defensive. A sentence such as, "you've made a mess all over the floor and I'm really cross," tells your toddler

that you are cross with him, not cross about the mess. Because he won't like what he is hearing, he is likely to tune out. If he feels particularly threatened and upset he may even have a full-blown tantrum.

Instead, try to use sentences that begin with "I." This lets you express your feelings without making your toddler feel that you are attacking him. A sentence such as, "I am feeling cross because there is a mess all over the floor that needs to be cleared up," places the emphasis on the mess rather than your toddler.

Listening to your toddler

Encourage your child to express himself through words, especially if his more natural choice of expression is hitting or throwing things. Ask him to stop his aggressive actions and encourage better communication by suggesting words to help him encompass his feelings – "you must be very angry that your car is broken," for example. This lets your child know you understand how he feels and offers him an alternative way to express his anger and frustration.

Listening to your child isn't just about hearing what he says, it is also about showing your child that you value what he has to say and that his opinion is important. If you don't give your child the attention he feels he deserves when he is talking to you, he is likely to resort to bad behavior to gain it. Things are likely to be much easier for both of you if he knows from the way you behave that you are interested. Try to look him in the face when you talk to him and, if necessary, get down to his height so that you can make eye-to-eye contact.

Try to find time each day for a family gathering where you all sit together and talk, perhaps at breakfast or another meal.

Negotiation

Older toddlers may use a request to do a thing they don't want to do as a bargaining tool. "If I put my shoes away will you let me have a cookie?" is one example of a toddler's bargaining strategy. Of course, you can't always comply with this – nor should you. Too much bribery can give the impression that everything is open to negotiation, which undermines your attempts to set firm limits. But don't dismiss it out of hand.

Sometimes bargaining can be a useful way to get your child to agree to requests that you know are especially tiresome for him. On these occasions, you may want to suggest a deal yourself rather than wait for your child to propose it. This way bargaining becomes a useful form of exchange that you both can benefit from.

Negative reactions

You can't always expect your toddler to communicate effectively. Sometimes, he may simply ignore you or pretend that he hasn't heard what you said. At other times he may try to argue with every suggestion, request or instruction you make. This type of behavior can be extremely wearing. You want to encourage your toddler to discuss his feelings constructively, but not to argue with everything you say.

If you feel your toddler has a genuine grievance, do try to modify your demands accordingly – or at least show him that you are prepared to listen. And if you feel he genuinely doesn't understand why he has to do something, always explain the reasons behind your demands. But don't allow your toddler to use argument simply as a way to prevaricate or resist your demands. If he is simply being difficult, you will need to stand firm.

learning about consequences

However you choose to discipline your child, your ultimate aim should be to teach your toddler how to discipline and control himself. The most effective way to get your toddler to take responsibility for his own behavior is to teach him that his actions have consequences.

Natural consequences

If your toddler is to learn to appreciate the way that his actions affect himself and others around him, he will need a certain amount of freedom to make his own choices and decisions – as well as his own mistakes. Your toddler may refuse to wear his gloves, for example, even though it is chilly outside. Explain to him that his hands will get cold but try to resist the temptation to force him to wear them. This way your toddler will learn from experience that the natural consequence of refusing to wear gloves is cold hands. No harm has been done, but he has learned a valuable lesson.

Parental intervention

Of course, there will be occasions when your toddler's actions have the potential to place him, or others, in danger – in these cases some form of intervention is vital. If your toddler wants to touch the fire, for example, you obviously need to prevent him from doing so. But you also need to explain to him why it is not allowed – because the fire will burn him – so that he understands what the consequences would have been.

Sometimes, parental intervention is necessary because the natural consequences of a certain type of misbehavior will not be immediately obvious to your toddler, such as when your child behaves aggressively toward another child. You may need to use some other form of discipline, such as giving time out (see page 70), to reinforce his awareness of the consequences of this bad behavior. If you do have to intervene, it is essential to communicate to your toddler why you have done so. This way he knows exactly why this behavior is not suitable and understands how to improve.

Pre-meditated discipline

For this type of parental intervention to be effective, the method of discipline you intend to use needs to have been thought through and fully explained to your toddler. If you've decided to use time out as a way to deal with aggression, for example, your child needs to understand that

> ## LOGICAL DISCIPLINE
>
> Whenever we went out, Suzy used to love chucking her toys in all directions. However much I told her off, she simply wasn't interested in picking them up. Eventually I told her that if she threw a toy away, she wouldn't get it back again. Every time she abandoned a toy I put it in a separate bag and refused to let her have it back. She soon realized the logic of picking up her toys herself.

Toddlers have limited powers of empathy and may not appreciate how upsetting selfish or aggressive behavior may be to others. In this case, you may need to intervene to make your toddler aware that his behavior does have consequences.

hitting or pushing another child will always result in time out – this way he knows that the consequences are inevitable. Consistency is all-important, as your child has to learn very early on that aggression is never going to be acceptable.

Immediate discipline

If you do intend to discipline your toddler for bad behavior, an immediate response is usually the best course of action. Young children live very much in the present and they may have difficulty connecting a delayed consequence with the original misdemeanor. If your child misbehaves while you are out, for example, don't wait to discipline him until you get home – your child is likely to have forgotten all about the incident. It's much better to warn him that you will take him home if he doesn't behave, then immediately do so if he continues to be difficult. This will help him connect his bad behavior with the consequences.

Appropriate discipline

One of the best ways to help your toddler appreciate the consequences of his actions is to ensure that the punishment fits the crime. If your toddler makes a mess during dinner, get him to help you clear the mess up. If he steals a cookie from the cupboard let him go without when you give his sister one. This way he can see that his punishment is a logical consequence of his behavior. On the other hand, you should never respond to your toddler's bad behavior by simply repeating it – spanking your child if he hits a friend risks reinforcing violent behavior rather than teaching him why it is wrong.

why spanking doesn't work

This is a very emotive issue and one about which a lot of parents, child welfare organizations and religious groups still disagree. Many adults believe that spanking is not effective and that adults have no right to inflict physical punishment on children. Others argue that they were spanked as children without it doing them any harm and they should be free to give their child a light smack on the bottom if he misbehaves. Even governments have difficulties in agreeing on this type of corporal punishment, and some countries – such as Sweden – have banned it altogether.

Sweden's rate for infant deaths at the hands of parents is now close to zero.

Although a spank or a slap may put a stop to undesirable behavior at the time, it does nothing to teach your child self-control, nor will it make your child behave well in the long term. And there is, of course, the very real risk of injuring your child if you hit him too hard.

Reasons to avoid spanking

As pain isn't a natural consequence of bad behavior, inflicting it on your child through a slap or a smack on the bottom doesn't teach him why his behavior is wrong. When he has been spanked, your child is much more likely to feel angry or resentful than to feel sorry for what he has done. There is even a risk that, as he gets older, he will learn to lie and be deceitful about things he has done wrong to avoid physical punishment.

Setting a good example

It is important to remember that your child learns by example and, as his parent, you are the most influential role model his life. Inflicting pain on your child to stop him misbehaving will simply teach him to solve his problems using violence.

A toddler who simply won't behave can make even the most calm and reasonable parent want to lash out. But spanking your child is never the right way to get your point across.

If he sees that you respond to feelings of anger or frustration by lashing out, he will find it difficult to learn other more acceptable and effective ways to deal with these feelings.

If you show your child that it is all right for you to use physical violence on him, he will think it must be all right for him to use it on others, too. You will teach him that it is fine for bigger or older people to hit smaller people. If you use spanking on a regular basis your child may grow up to become a bully, or he may become the victim and be bullied.

Controlling yourself

Even though most parents know and understand all the reasons not to spank their children, very few manage to make it all the way through the toddler years without administering a slap in the heat of the moment. When you get very angry with your child the adrenaline pumps through your body, triggering the "fight or flight" response and making it difficult not to lose your composure. Often, the slap occurs as a result of a long series of annoyances and is precipitated by

Children who receive physical punishment from their parents often respond by taking out their aggression on younger or weaker siblings or playmates.

something very trivial that becomes the last straw. This release of anger may help you for a brief moment, but the guilt soon sets in at the sight of your child's tears and you give him a hug. Not only does this teach him that aggression is acceptable, it may also cause you both to lose sight of the original misdemeanor.

If you do lose your cool and lash out in anger, the best thing you can do is apologize to your child for hurting him and explain what it was about his behavior that made you so angry that you lost your temper. You need to make him understand why you hit him this time, but also that this doesn't make physical violence right.

WATCH **POINT...**

SHAKING

Never shake your toddler, no matter how angry or frustrated you may feel. Young children have, proportionally, much heavier heads than adults and weaker neck muscles. Their brains are still immature and more easily injured and the blood vessels around their brains are more susceptible to tearing. Shaking can cause serious injuries including brain damage and blindness.

rewarding your toddler

The distinction between a bribe and a reward is a very subtle one. It could be said that a bribe is something offered to induce good behavior, while a reward is a bonus given when your child behaves well without the need to coerce him. In practice, the difference is usually one of degree, not kind. Rewarding good behavior is generally preferable to bribing your child, but there may well be a place for both in your armory of disciplinary techniques.

What to offer

Adults often assume that a reward for good behavior needs to be something tangible, such as a sticker or a small toy. But most young toddlers are as happy with a big smile or a hug – your praise and attention is reward enough.

Older toddlers and pre-school children are more aware of the material value of things. Although they still want praise, they are likely to appreciate something more tangible. Don't go overboard – rewards shouldn't cost a fortune. Try to avoid offering your toddler cookies or candy as a reward as this can encourage unhealthy eating habits. You will also need to give your child his reward immediately – making him wait to receive his prize won't work, as toddlers have difficulty understanding the concept of delayed gratification.

Making a chart

One way to encourage ongoing good behavior is to use a chart and stickers. You could give your child a sticker every time he tidies his toys away and offer a bigger reward, such as a small toy or a trip to the park, once he has earned five or ten stickers. For this to work, you need to make it clear to your child what he has to do to earn a sticker and how many stickers he has to get to earn a more tangible prize.

It's also important to remember that this is a reward scheme, so you mustn't remove stickers if your toddler behaves badly or refuses to do what is expected of him. The intention is to reward his good behavior, not to draw attention to his naughtiness.

CHILD'S PLAY

Lucky dip
Keep a bag full of small, inexpensive items that you know your toddler likes. Then, when he has been especially good, get him to close his eyes and pull an item out. The anticipation and suspense will make the reward even more exciting.

4 Tantrums and triggers

A tantrum is an emotional outburst that occurs when your toddler feels out of control. It is not always simply a show of temper – it can also be an expression of the frustration your toddler feels at her physical or mental inability to achieve what she wants. Understanding and avoiding the things that trigger your toddler's tantrums can go a long way toward preventing them.

early tantrums

Young babies may cry a lot, but they don't really have tantrums: this type of unrestrained outburst of rage and emotion – complete with kicking, screaming and bawling – is a particular characteristic of toddlerhood. Some children start having tantrums as early as 18 months, others don't start until they are over two years old – whatever age they first occur, tantrums are a perfectly normal part of your toddler's development. They can be distressing for you both, but they also provide an vital outlet for your toddler's frustrations.

Sometimes an approaching tantrum is easy to spot; at other times it may blow up without warning and for no apparent reason. Tantrums usually last no longer than three or four minutes at a time and generally end as quickly as they begin. Once the tantrum is over, your toddler will recover very quickly and within minutes she may be back to her normal, smiling self – as though nothing has happened.

Tantrums rarely last long at this age. When they are over you will need to be there for your toddler to show him you still love him.

What are tantrums?

Your toddler's first tantrums occur as an almost instinctive reaction to a particularly frustrating or upsetting situation – they should certainly not be seen as a premeditated show of temper or an act of defiance. Very often, these tantrums are connected to your toddler's relationship with you. At this age, she is still struggling to reconcile her continuing reliance on you with an increasing desire to be independent. She wants to please you but she also needs to defy you.

Don't be surprised if your child turns on you during a tantrum, pushing you away, kicking out at you, or even running away from you. She won't actually want to go too far and she probably won't let you out of her sight, so don't be too alarmed. Sometimes, younger toddlers throw themselves on the ground, yell and scream, or even drum their feet on the ground for added effect. Again, your toddler doesn't actually want you to leave her, she is just testing the limits of her relationship with you.

Your toddler has very little control over these early tantrums, although she will probably give you some warning that they are about to happen. Many of these early tantrums can be avoided by distracting your toddler before she really gets going – see pages 56–62 for advice on avoiding some of the most common triggers.

How should you react?

These early tantrums are usually over very quickly and are easy to put behind you and maybe even laugh about. While they are happening, you need to allow your child the space to push away from you, if that is what she wants to do, but be ready to welcome her back when it's all over. Your toddler needs to know that she has your unconditional love, even though it may seem as though she doesn't want it. Don't be tempted to withdraw your affection because

your child has withdrawn hers: she needs the reassurance of knowing that you are always there for her, even when she is behaving badly.

Tantrum-free toddlers

There will always be some parents who tell you that their children never have tantrums. Unlikely as this may seem – especially if yours is a two- or three-tantrums-a-day child – it is possible. Children's behavior varies, as do the reactions of parents to this behavior. What one parent considers to be a tantrum, another may simply interpret as an upset. Other parents see tantrums as a sign of failure on their part and prefer not to admit to their toddler having them.

tantrums in older toddlers

As your toddler grows older, you will probably start to notice that her tantrums last a little longer. She may also take longer to recover from these more developed tantrums. Your older toddler should now be much more aware that she is behaving badly – although she still finds it very hard to control herself – and this may make her scared and sorry when it's all over.

Stages to watch for

As well as lasting longer, an older toddler's tantrums may have a more identifiable structure and you may start to recognize distinct stages:

● First there is a pre-tantrum stage when your toddler makes it obvious that she is spoiling for a fight and wants you to challenge her so that she

has an excuse. Ask her to do something and she may respond with a cheeky "No, you do it."

● If you try and force the issue, you give her the perfect excuse (as far as she is concerned) to move onto the next stage. This usually involves screaming and shouting, which may be accompanied by stamping of feet, hitting out or even breaking things.

● Some toddlers follow this up by hurling themselves on the floor or banging their heads against something hard so that they actually bruise and hurt themselves. Make sure your toddler doesn't seriously injure herself, but don't be too alarmed by her behavior – it doesn't mean she has psychological problems and most toddlers grow out of the phase quite quickly.

Tantrums can be very difficult to ignore, especially if your child throws herself about the room. Make sure she is safe but resist the temptation to fuss – you don't want to make a big deal out of her behavior.

● Finally, there is the winding down stage when your toddler's anger is spent and her screams gradually turn into tears and whimpers. This is when your toddler really needs you.

How should you react?

By their very nature, tantrums are difficult to ignore and you are likely to get very wound up by your toddler's behavior. To remain calm, you need to take some deep breaths or even walk away – but be ready to hold and cuddle your child when the tantrum has ended. You may find that she wants to be near you but refuses to be held   this is all right, too. Give her the space to regain her self-control and wait for her to come to you. Tantrums that go on for more than a few minutes – some toddlers can keep a tantrum going for anything up to an hour – will need different coping strategies (see pages 74–77).

When your toddler has calmed down, you will need to comfort and reassure her – she is likely to feel very shaken by her anger. When she is in a more reasonable frame of mind, you could try suggesting some more acceptable ways for her to manage her frustrations – by asking you for help earlier, for example, or by trying to use words to express how she feels. Don't expect her to get the hang of all this yet, though, she needs time to learn control. Avoid lecturing her or blaming her for her behavior.

Outgrowing tantrums

By the age of four most toddlers will have outgrown their tantrums and should have learned that there are better ways to get what they want. However, some children continue until school age and beyond. If your child is one of these, she may be acting this way because she thinks that tantrums will get her something she wants – perhaps you or your partner have given in to her tantrums in the past.

If your toddler is still tantruming at this age you need to work out whether she has any control over herself. Look for her watching you out of the corner of her eye or stopping and starting the fuss depending on whether you are taking any notice of her. Even if you are sure that she is deliberately using tantrums to get her own way, this doesn't make her scheming. She has simply learned what works for her and is using this to achieve her own ends. You have to show her that tantrums don't work and that there are other ways of getting what she wants, such as verbally expressing her needs or anger (see page 76).

common tantrum triggers

You may come to recognize that certain situations and places are particularly likely to trigger your toddler's tantrums. It would be great if you could simply avoid these situations altogether, but it is unlikely this will always be possible. Even if you can manage to keep your toddler away from places such as the supermarket – a common tantrum hotspot – the emotional trigger factors behind tantrums can be much more difficult to control.

Your toddler may have a tantrum because she wants your undivided attention at a moment when you can't give it to her. She may be feeling upset because she is hungry, tired, unwell or bored. Or she may simply be frustrated by the limitations of being a toddler. These emotional triggers have the potential to cause tantrums at any time, but there are certain situations when they are particularly likely to cause a problem. An awareness of these situations and of some of the ways to manage your toddler, should help you to avoid too many tantrums.

DIFFICULT SITUATIONS

- Trips to the store, especially the supermarket
- Arriving at or leaving the playgroup or nursery
- Leaving your toddler to go to work
- Bedtimes and bathtimes
- Dressing or undressing your toddler
- Mealtimes

Supermarkets and shopping

Tantrums while you are out shopping can be a real pain, especially if they occur in the queue for the checkout when you are surrounded by people. Before you start feeling bad about your inability to control your child, it is worth remembering that supermarkets have all the ingredients necessary to provoke a tantrum in any toddler – noise, bustle and an array of items

> ## NEGOTIATION
>
> Mark had been fine until we got to the aisle where the candies were. I'd already told him we weren't buying any candy today, but he decided to throw the most spectacular tantrum to try to make me change my mind. It would have been so easy to give in for the sake of peace, but I knew if I did it would happen every time we came to the store. In the end I managed to bribe him with the promise of a go on the coin-operated ride outside the store when we were finished.

that your child wants but can't have. All this, plus the fact you are distracted, adds up to a sure-fire recipe for a major tantrum. And if your toddler is over the age of three, don't think she hasn't worked this out for herself.

Preventing tantrums

Avoid shopping at times when you know your toddler will need a nap or will get hungry, since this is when tantrums are most likely to occur. If you can't avoid going shopping at these times, take along a pushchair for your toddler to nap in or some healthy snacks to keep her happy.

If you know that a tantrum is on its way, try to distract your toddler. Involve her in the choices you make about your purchases, talk to her about what you are going to do when you get home or take the opportunity to teach her about the things you see. Speed up your trip so that she doesn't have too much time to get bored. Toddlers have limited patience for shopping, and once this has expired there's little you can do but cut your losses and go home.

When you've made your way to the checkout, don't give in to pleas for candy or treats while you are waiting to pay. If the tantrum develops into a full-blown drama, tell your child that her behavior isn't acceptable and take her home without further ado, even if it means cutting your shopping trip short.

Avoid tantrums when you are out shopping by keeping your toddler busy. Set him tasks or get him to help carry things for you. If you view your shopping trip as an adventure instead of a chore you will both have a lot more fun.

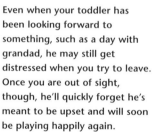

Even when your toddler has been looking forward to something, such as a day with grandad, he may still get distressed when you try to leave. Once you are out of sight, though, he'll quickly forget he's meant to be upset and will soon be playing happily again.

Beginnings and endings

Tantrums often occur at the start or end of events. They may be triggered by your attempts to get your toddler to finish doing something she enjoys – when you want her to stop playing and get out of the bath, for example. Or they may occur when you want her to start something she doesn't want to do. But it isn't just her likes or dislikes that cause the problems; it is often the transition itself that she objects to. Even when you know she is really excited about going to see a friend or a favorite relative, for example, she may still have a tantrum when you try to make her leave the house.

The major problem here is that toddlers find it very hard to cope with change. Anything that involves a change in circumstances – especially if it involves being separated from you – can be very upsetting for your child.

Toddlers live very much in the present. They have little conception of time and little appreciation for the demands of a busy adult schedule. When they are doing something they enjoy, they quickly become emotionally and intellectually engaged. You may know that your toddler will be just as happy once she starts something new, but she won't understand why she should have to stop what she is doing.

Problems at home

Very occasionally your toddler may continue her tantrums after the start or end of a situation. This may be because of insecurity she is feeling at home – perhaps there is some marital tension between you and your partner or maybe there's been a recent house move or a death in the family. Stress within the family often means a toddler gets less attention, so she feels insecure and unsure of her position within the family group. Tantrums are a way of demanding attention and asking for reassurance.

How should you react?

If you know that your toddler finds the transition between activities very difficult, make sure you give her plenty of warning. Tell her ten minutes or so before you want her to do something, so she has plenty of time to prepare for and adjust to the change in activities.

Toddlers require lots of repetition and practice before they become attuned to the rhythms of adult lives. Consistent, predictable routines will help your toddler plan for and predict changes.

Leaving for work

If you are a working parent, you may well be familiar with the guilt your child can provoke by throwing a tantrum whenever you try to leave. This misery is unlikely to be because she is unhappy about your childcare arrangements – although you should consider this possibility. It is much more likely that your toddler is genuinely anxious about being separated from you. Her tears won't last and she should grow out of her anxiety in time. In the meantime, all you can do is be firm but kind and not drag leavings out unnecessarily. For more detailed advice on dealing with separation anxiety, see pages 84–85.

> ## " SAYING GOODBYE
>
> Florence loves my mum and is always excited about going to see her. Sometimes I try to leave them together while I go shopping, but from my daughter's reaction you'd think I was inflicting the worst kind of punishment on her. One day, after a particularly traumatic parting, I crept back up the drive and peeped through the window. There was Florence happily sitting on her grandma's knee while they looked through a picture book together. There wasn't a tear in sight. "

Dressing and undressing

This area of toddlercare is often fraught with difficulties. Your toddler may love the challenge of getting herself dressed and undressed and she may be perfectly happy for you do it for her. Alternatively – and this is very common – she'll fight you all the way.

Tantrums over your choice of clothes are typical – you want your toddler to look smart and to dress appropriately for the weather, but she wants to wear her favorite scruffy jumper that's two sizes too small and her old dungarees with a tear in their seat. You're then faced with a choice between triggering a tantrum and having a child who looks like a ragbag.

Another problem area can be the length of time it takes to get dressed. If your child is slow or easily distracted, the time it takes to get her ready can be a source of irritation for you both, especially first thing in the morning when you are in a hurry to get out of the house. The more you cajole her to hurry up, the slower she will become. If you try to intervene she may have a tantrum because she doesn't want your help; if you get angry with her or lose your temper she'll just get even more upset.

How should you react?

If you sense a battle over getting dressed coming on, you could try sitting down with your toddler and explaining why she needs to hurry up or why she can't wear a summer skirt and a T-shirt when it's snowing outside. If this doesn't work, and your child refuses to hurry up or has a full-blown tantrum, there is nothing else for it but to pick her and her clothes up and take her to the front door. Finish getting her dressed there so that she understands that going out is the next step.

If your toddler wants to wear unsuitable clothing or refuses to put on certain items, such as a coat or gloves when it's cold, let her learn from experience how wearing the wrong clothes or going out without these items will affect her. If there are clothes you really don't want her to wear, pick out a few different options so that she has a choice about what she can put on.

" CHOOSING FOR HERSELF

Lucy had some really lovely little dresses, but for some reason she completely went off wearing them. Every morning I selected something pretty, but she refused to put it on. If I insisted, she had a tantrum. If I gave in and let her choose, on the other hand, she stopped playing up very quickly. Now I offer her a choice of three outfits and, as she knows that it has to be one of these, she chooses what to wear without too much fuss.

Tantrum-free dressing

- ✓ If the weather where you live is very seasonal, put away all the previous season's clothes when the weather starts to change

- ✓ Offer your toddler a choice of clothes, but make it limited

- ✓ Allow more time for your toddler to get dressed by getting up ten minutes earlier

- ✓ Encourage your child to dress himself, but be on hand in case he has a problem

- ✓ Don't laugh at or criticize your toddler's efforts to dress himself

- ✓ Remember that socks and shoes can be difficult for a toddler to put on, so be ready to help when he gets stuck

Your toddler may object to getting undressed at the end of the day because this heralds bedtime. She may be anxious about being separated from you or afraid of the dark, or she may just want to carry on playing. If trying to get her into her nightdress results in a tantrum, you could always put her into bed in the clothes she is wearing.

Mealtimes

All sorts of things can trigger tantrums during mealtimes. If your toddler is hungry she will become ratty, just as adults do. Trying to make her eat food that she doesn't want, or not letting her have a food that she does want, will provoke a similar reaction. If you tell her off for playing with her food, or try to make her stay at the table when she wants to go, a tantrum can result.

In addition, certain rituals, that often only your toddler understands, can cause food refusal and a tantrum. She might be upset that a piece of meat is touching the potatoes, that her sandwiches are cut into squares and not triangles, or that the meal is not on her favorite plate. This type of ritual may seem ridiculous to you, but it can be very important to your toddler.

How you should react

As it's so easy to get it wrong with your toddler at mealtimes, it's probably best to go along with as many of her whims as you can. If she doesn't like yogurts with bits in, for example, offer her smooth yogurt instead – it's just as good and certainly not worth having a battle over.

Forcing your toddler to eat something she doesn't want to eat is a sure-fire route to a tantrum. Try to be flexible and avoid starting battles unless absolutely necessary.

Of course, you need to stand firm over the important things, such as deliberately upending her dish onto the floor, or spitting food out. You also need to act when safety becomes an issue – if your child runs around while eating, for example, she might make herself choke. When faced with a tantrum over food refusal, try to remember that your toddler won't starve herself. Even if she only eats crisps and cookies for a period, these do have some nutritional value. See page 30 for more advice on dealing with food refusal.

On the phone

Like many parents, you may find that your toddler always seems to wait until the moment you pick up the phone before deciding that she urgently needs you for something. Whatever she wants won't wait until you've finished talking – if you ask her to wait, or try to ignore her, she'll

soon start making so much noise that further conversation is almost impossible. If your toddler often behaves like this it is probably because she wants your undivided attention and resents anything that seems to come between you.

How should you react?

Ask your caller to hold while you explain to your toddler that you need some time to make this call. Tell her that she needs to amuse herself for a few minutes until you finish. Give her some suggestions of things that she could do, such as playing with a certain toy or getting her boots on so that you can go out when you've finished, and limit the time you spend on the phone.

It may help to have a portable phone so that you can do things with, or for, your toddler while you are talking on the phone. If she knows you haven't forgotten her, she is less likely to behave in a way that demands all of your attention.

When you have finished your call, don't forget to praise your toddler, if she has been playing quietly, and tell her what a help she has been.

Avoid simply ignoring your toddler when you are talking on the phone. This way, although he doesn't have your undivided attention, he doesn't feel that it has been completely withdrawn.

5 Tantrum strategies

Tantrums are a perfectly normal part of your toddler's development, but there are ways to make them less frequent – or at least a little less overwhelming for you both. Although there is no guaranteed way to prevent tantrums occurring, a few pre-planned diversionary tactics or distractions should help you avoid the worst. And when a tantrum does occur, there are strategies to help you contain or manage the outburst until your child is able to regain control of his feelings.

giving your toddler structure

One of the most effective strategies for avoiding tantrums is to provide your toddler with plenty of routine in his life. Although toddlers often seem chaotic and unruly, they do like the comfort and security that a structured existence gives them. Your toddler will be happiest if his day is planned so that he has routines that are familiar to him. This way he always knows exactly what to expect.

Structuring his day in this way gives your toddler less opportunity to get wound up about unexpected events and less reason to whine when he has to start doing something new. If he knows that he always has to do something at a certain time each day he is less likely to kick up a fuss – he will accept that having a tantrum is unlikely to change your mind. It also will help you to plan your day better, helping to minimize last minute panics and tantrums caused by your subsequent attempts to rush your toddler along.

Striking the right balance

Providing a good routine for your child does not mean occupying every hour of his day with organized activities. Too much structure and stimulation can leave a child feeling that he's unable to live up to other people's expecations. This may make him stressed or anxious – which

Setting a structured nightime routine will prepare your toddler and help her settle more easily at nights – many parents like to provide a healthy snack and a drink before bedtime.

is also likely to lead to tears and tantrums. A good weekly routine should provide your child with the security and the space he needs to be able to explore things for himself. There should be a good balance between structured activities and unstructured play and, most importantly, it should be clear to your toddler when it is time to move from one to the other. It shouldn't block your toddler's natural spontaneity and creativity.

Creating your routine

Try to lay down routines that your child can associate with certain times of his day. For example, you could insist that mealtimes are always taken sitting at the table or that bathtime is always followed by a cuddle and a story, and then bed. Regular, structured mealtimes and bedtimes have the additional benefit of helping ensure that your toddler doesn't get too hungry or too tired – both of which are very common causes of tantrums.

Young children have short memories, so frequent reminders are needed about what you want your toddler to do and how you expect him to behave. Be careful, however, that these reminders don't turn into nagging and that they are not said in such a way that your child sees them as frequent criticism. Nagging and criticism are likely to make your child's behavior worse and will do nothing to help him build his self-esteem (see page 12).

Creating boundaries

An essential part of the structure of a child's life, boundaries are needed while your child is learning to develop self-control. He may still try to test the limits of these boundaries, but he is less likely to feel aggrieved or have a tantrum when you try to stop him.

To allow your child to explore and challenge limits without putting himself in danger, these

> ## SHE NEEDS A ROUTINE
>
> Even when she was a baby Tara used to get into a real state if her routine was changed. Now she's a toddler, she is even worse. She has to have her own bowl and cutlery and she always sits on the same chair at mealtimes. Sometimes her big brother tries to sit in her place and she absolutely hits the roof. She is fine when we go out – It's only at home that she wants everything to be kept the same.

boundaries often need to be physical. If you allow your child to play in the garden, but forbid him to go out through the front gate, at some point he will forget your instruction and he will open the gate. If you put a bolt or chain on the gate this will ensure that he stays within the boundary you have set and avoid the row and potential danger that could ensue when he ventures outside.

distraction and diversion

It is sometimes possible to head off a tantrum simply by distracting your toddler – especially since boredom often plays a role in events. If your child is showing all the signs of building up to an outburst, take his mind off things by suggesting something exciting or interesting for him to do. This won't always work – some toddlers get even more angry if they feel that you are trying to divert their attention from what is bothering them – but it can be an effective way to defuse a tense situation.

Distracting your toddler

The more time and energy your toddler invests in his tantrum, and the more upset he starts to feel, the harder it will be to stop it getting worse. As soon as you see your toddler's bottom lip start to wobble or his brow start to furrow,

If you can see a tantrum approaching, but can't give your toddler your undivided attention, get him involved in what you are doing. This way you can distract him at the same time as getting on with your chores.

CAR-SEAT BATTLE

At about nine months, Lindy began to refuse to sit in her car seat. When I tried to make her there would be a big fuss and she would go rigid so that I couldn't sit her down. At first I managed to distract her by letting her have the car keys to play with or tickling her. But, as she got older I had to become much cleverer at finding ways to distract her and often had to resort to bribery.

you immediately need to draw his attention away from whatever seems to be upsetting him. Wait too long to act and you might miss your chance to nip his tantrum in the bud.

Perhaps you can get his attention by calling his name or some other word or phrase that will make him momentarily forget his objective. Call him over and tell him you have something to show him. Or try pointing out something around you that will interest him – a car that looks "just like mommy's," perhaps, a pretty bird in the garden or an airplane flying overhead. Make eye contact as you talk to him.

Diverting your toddler

As soon as you have managed to distract your toddler from whatever was bothering him, you will need to redirect his attention onto something that will keep him busy and occupied. If you are at home, you might suggest to your child that you read him a story, you could start playing a silly game or you could ask him to do something unexpected like helping you make

some cookies. If you are too busy to give him all of your attention, show him something he can do by himself such as painting a picture or watching a favorite video or DVD.

Sometimes, indulging in a boisterous game or encouraging your child to run, jump and dance to some loud music will stop a tantrum before it has the chance to become full-blown. Not only does this type of activity provide a distraction for your toddler, it also gives him a chance to work off some excess energy. You may find that it helps to join in. It doesn't matter so much what you suggest, so long as it provides a change of activity. You need to prevent his mind from going straight back onto whatever was bothering him in the first place.

Pre-emptive action

This type of strategy is most effective when used as a prevention, rather than a cure. Try to anticipate potential tantrum situations and, when you think that a certain situation might cause a problem, provide your child plenty of diversions. If you take your toddler with you when you go to the store, for example, involve him in your decisions, point out different objects and ask him about colors and shapes. If you are lucky, this should keep him busy for long enough to make it home without too much fuss

If your toddler does start whining about being bored, or demanding items that you don't want to buy, your best move is to get out as quickly as possible and head for home.

humor and games

Getting your child to laugh is one of the most effective ways to diffuse a tantrum. Once you've got your toddler giggling he'll find it very difficult to remain cross or miserable. As most children much prefer to laugh rather than cry, raising a smile shouldn't be too difficult.

Young children love slapstick humor – funny faces, big gestures and silly voices will all make them dissolve into fits of giggles. As soon as your child looks as though he's about to have a tantrum, turn yourself into a clown so that he starts to focus on you rather than on the problem that is making him miserable. If you can keep up the performance for long enough, he is likely to completely forget what was upsetting him and you will avoid the tantrum.

" TEDDY TO THE RESCUE

When Ben got upset I would discuss the situation with 'teddy,' Ben's favorite toy. We would have a conversation, with me using different voices, about what we thought the problem that was making Ben unhappy might be. Very often Ben would become so interested in what was being said that he would join in too and we were able to resolve the problem without a fuss. "

Playing games

A good way to put the smile back on your toddler's face is to turn boring chores into fun games. If it's pouring down outside but your child is refusing point blank to wear his rubber boots, you could tell him that if he puts them on you will take him to find some puddles to jump in – suggest that you see who can make the biggest splash. Most toddlers would find this offer hard to resist. The boots will soon go on and the two of you will share some fun as you splash through the puddles together.

There are lots of other games you can try – use your imagination and just go with the flow! Although heading off a tantrum with fun and games can sometimes feel like hard work, it can be well worth the effort. You are likely to be rewarded with a happy, smiling child.

Bets and challenges

A great way to get your toddler to do a boring task a little quicker or more willingly is to make it into a competition – your toddler will love the opportunity to beat you or to prove you wrong. You could try betting him that he can't put his shoes on all by himself or challenging him to a race to see who can tidy up the toys in one half of the room the fastest.

Only race your toddler if you don't mind him being a bit slapdash in whatever he is doing – at this age you can't really expect him to be quick and neat. And don't try too hard to win or he'll simply get discouraged. With a bit of luck, your toddler will have so much fun he won't even realize that the same task provoked a tantrum last time you tried it.

The smile inspector

Toddlers find it difficult to resist a bit of reverse psychology. Instead of telling your sulky toddler to cheer up, try telling her to make sure she doesn't smile. Look her straight in the face and as soon as you detect even a hint of a smirk announce, 'whoops, I can see a smile...' She should start to grin in spite of herself, and you can cry, 'yes, there it is!' and give her a big hug. This trick doesn't work every time, but it's worth a try now and then.

Make believe

You may want to involve the help of a favorite toy, such as a teddy bear or a doll, to win your toddler round. By adopting different voices you can give them different characters and use them to suggest ideas that he might reject coming straight from you. Having teddy suggest that your child is feeling sleepy and it is time for bed is more likely to appeal to a toddler who is feeling cross and fractious than the same request coming from an adult.

If you are feeling particularly imaginative, you can create imaginary storylines to make boring jobs seem more exciting. If you are trying on new shoes, for example, get your toddler to imagine she is Snow White putting on a crystal slipper – tell her that the shoe has to fit perfectly if she is to find her handsome prince.

When to keep a straight face

You do need to be careful how you introduce humor into a stressful situation. Your toddler can be very sensitive, and it's important not to give the impression that you are laughing at him or making fun of his feelings – no one likes to feel they are not being taken seriously. You may find your toddler absolutely adorable when he's angry, but it certainly won't help to show him. You need to respect his concerns and show him that you understand why he is upset.

In some cases, laughing at your toddler's bad behavior could actually encourage him to repeat it. It can be hard not to show your amusement when your little angel uses a rude word that he clearly doesn't understand, or tries to tell you he hasn't eaten any chocolate when he has the evidence smeared all around his mouth. But doing so may encourage your toddler to play up to his audience. Then, when you tire of his new party trick and try to tell him to stop, he won't understand why it is no longer funny – the perfect recipe for a tantrum.

time out

This is a very good strategy to help calm things down when a tantrum is brewing. It is also an effective way to stop a tantrum that is in full swing because it allows all the parties involved – usually you and your child – a chance to cool off.

Time out means giving your child the time and space he needs to regain his self-control. You can do this by removing your child from center stage and placing him somewhere where his antics can be ignored. Or, if you prefer, you can walk away yourself. The purpose is not to punish your child but to separate him from the situation or person that is upsetting him so that he has the opportunity to calm down. It will also help you avoid becoming too wound up by his behavior while you wait for this to happen. It's a good idea to work out what type of behavior warrants time out before the situation arises – if the strategy is used too often it loses its impact. Many parents keep time out in reserve for when their child behaves particularly badly – hitting or hurting others, for example, breaking things, or losing control.

Time-out techniques

The most important factor in any time-out procedure is to remain calm and in control. If you shout, argue, or act irrationally you will be behaving in the same way as your toddler and the situation will only get worse.

Gently but firmly placing your toddler in the time-out chair will give you both the opportunity to calm down – but don't use it too often or it will lose impact.

When your toddler reaches a stage of behavior that you feel is no longer acceptable, tell him that he needs time out, explain to him why he needs it, and then carry out whichever time-out procedure you have decided works best. Common techniques include taking your toddler to a time-out room or putting him in a particular chair to calm down.

Using a time-out room

Your child's bedroom is probably the most appropriate time-out room because you know it is a safe place for him to be left in. If your child has persistent sleep problems you may want to consider using another room in the house or another time-out method, as you don't want him to come to associate his room with punishment.

When you want your toddler to have time out, take him by the hand, or carry him if you have to, and put him in his room. Be gentle but firm, and use a tone of voice that brooks no argument. If you sound as though you might waver your child will immediately pick up on this and try and use it to his advantage. Once you have told him that he has to stay there until he has calmed

down, you should leave the room, shut the door and move quickly away from the scene.

If your child is an escape artist who manages to get out of his room before you've had time to turn around, take him back and tell him again that he must stay there until he is calmer. You may have to do this several times, but don't be tempted to give in or your child will view time out as an empty threat. However frequently your toddler escapes, don't be tempted to lock the bedroom door as this is only likely to frighten your child.

Using a time-out chair

Some children, especially those who become even more furious and uncooperative if they are left on their own, respond well to a chair set aside in the corner of a room. It may help to set a timer, and to tell your child that he must sit there until it goes off. Other than that, this

> ### " EFFECTIVE TIME OUT
>
> Robyn was having a full-blown tantrum so I put her in her room and then waited outside to see if she would calm down. Of course, she knew I was still there and played up accordingly. Now when I use time out I shut the door firmly and walk away. It works every time. "

You may find that, having ensured that your toddler is safe where he is, removing yourself from the scene is more effective in calming things down.

method of time out requires much the same techniques as using the bedroom. Be firm and tell your child that he must sit on the chair until he is calm.

This method doesn't work well for every child. If you find it difficult to get your child to remain seated on the chair it may even exacerbate an already tense situation. Do not allow it to become a battle between you or it will become a no-win situation – you will get more angry and your child's behavior will get even worse. In this event you will need to try another method.

Walking away

Removing yourself from the scene, rather than your toddler, can also be an effective time-out technique, providing you do it calmly and quietly. By ignoring your toddler and walking away, you both give him the space he needs to recover himself and deprive him of his audience. This is also useful in situations when you feel unable to control your own temper.

Tell your child that you both need time out and that you are going to leave him until you have both calmed down. Then, having made sure that he is safe, leave the room and close the door firmly behind you. Do not leave after yelling at him or slam the door behind you – this will show that his tantrum has had a real affect on you, which may be just what he wanted.

What happens next

Most experts believe that time out should only last for the same number of minutes as your child's age – three minutes if he is three years old, and so on. You may still be feeling cross, but don't keep reminding your child about how naughty he has been or discuss his bad behavior in front of him. This will only maintain the tension between you both or draw attention to his tantrum and will probably succeed in making you both miserable.

Try to be calm and welcoming to your toddler. Say something like, "It's good to see you are so much calmer now," and then suggest that he joins you in some activity. Some children need a lot of reassurance after a tantrum, so a hug and a quick cuddle may be appropriate. Don't overdo it though – your child shouldn't be made to feel that he is being rewarded for his tantrum.

Being realistic about results

Time out isn't an instant solution for bad behavior – it's more like a safety valve for parent and child. Don't expect your child to come out of his room and apologize for his behavior or promise to be angelic from there on in. The best you can hope for is that your child will be in a more reasonable frame of mind and that this will last for a while. If he comes out of his room and immediately goes off into another tantrum, you must put him back firmly, explaining what you are doing and why.

Sometimes, a child will play quite happily during a time out, seemingly unconcerned about being sent to his room. This can be very irritating for a stressed out parent, but try to remember that the whole point of time out is to give you both space to calm down. What either of you do with this time is unimportant so long as the end result is the right one.

Coping with your anger

Even though your toddler has calmed down, you may still feel angry and frustrated at his behavior. It's fine to let him know how you feel – anger is not something you need to hide – but you do need to be in control of it. It can be good for your toddler to understand that his behavior can make you feel upset too.

Even if you do feel angry, don't be tempted to drag up all the other instances when your child has upset you in a similar way – he simply won't be able to cope with that. His memory is too short to remember the things he has done wrong in the past, so he'll just feel trapped and bewildered by your outburst.

> **" I NEED TIME OUT TOO**
>
> Sometimes Olivia makes me so mad I have to walk away otherwise I know there's a risk I might slap her. I have to take a deep breath and tell her that, 'I need time out because I am too cross to talk to you right now.' When I return to the room having calmed down, she nearly always comes and asks for a cuddle. It's as though she needs to be reassured that I still love her. **"**

hugging and holding

Some experts suggest that holding a child through a tantrum is the best way to help him control his anger and frustration. They believe that holding your wriggling, crying child against your body can give him security, help him control his inner rage, and provide somewhere safe where he can calm down. As your toddler starts to regain his self-control, the hold often turns into a comforting hug.

This theory certainly works for some parents and children, but it is not suitable for every child or in every situation. Some toddlers, particularly as they grow older, don't like being held. The feeling of constraint may make them even more frustrated. If this type of technique does not seem to work with your toddler, you may have to find other ways to deal with tantrums.

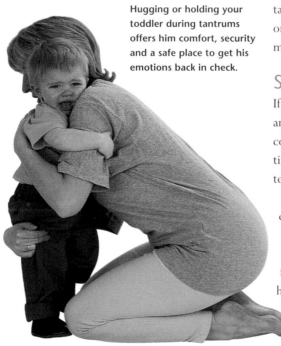

Hugging or holding your toddler during tantrums offers him comfort, security and a safe place to get his emotions back in check.

Holding also can be an effective technique if you find that your toddler doesn't otherwise seem to notice anything that you say to him during a tantrum. Physical contact – hugging, restraining, or even stroking your toddler – is a good way to make sure that you get his attention.

Staying in control

If you are going to attempt to hold a squirming, angry toddler you need to be very calm and in control of your own feelings. If you are already tired, overwrought and angry, this holding technique is probably not right for the situation.

You need to be able to hold your toddler firmly enough for him to feel secure, but not so strongly that he becomes powerless. If he's fighting mad he will certainly struggle to get free of you and there is a real risk of you holding him too firmly or even unintentionally hurting him. Of course, there is also a risk of him hurting you as he lashes out, and if you are not in control of your own emotions you may find yourself retaliating if anger gets the better of you. By staying calm and in control, you will communicate this calm to your toddler and show him how he should react.

Emotional cut off

If you feel that your toddler is using his tantrums as a way to get more attention, you may find it more effective to hold him without looking at him so that he can feel that you are there for him physically, but without all the warmth and affection he normally associates with being held in your arms. By withholding yourself in this way you will be denying your toddler the attention that he hopes his tantrum will gain. If you start soothing and stroking, your toddler may feel that his tantrum has achieved what he wanted and he will use this method again.

A hug hold

Most experts feel that it is the physical contact provided by being held by a familiar adult that an angry toddler finds most calming. Holding a child from behind in a close but gentle hug enables the parent or carer to get near to the toddler without running the risk of being kicked or punched or indeed provoking further kicking and punching. The idea is to embrace your child from the back, putting your arms around his chest so that you can hold him gently but firmly against you. This type of hold is especially useful if your toddler becomes violent during a tantrum and is likely to hurt himself or others.

Other ways to contain your toddler

You may feel that your child would benefit from some sort of restraint during his tantrums but prefer not to keep hold of him yourself – maybe you don't want to encourage attention-seeking tantrums; perhaps you don't trust yourself to stay calm when feelings are running high. If this is the case, you may find it more effective to strap your toddler into his buggy or place him in his highchair or playpen until he has calmed down. You will need to stay close to your child, as he will doubtless try to escape. Don't use this strategy too often, otherwise being put in the buggy, highchair or playpen will come to be seen as a kind of punishment.

The hug hold provides reassuring security, even if your toddler is violent during his tantrums. In this position you also can talk softly in his ear.

talking tactics

Most toddlers reach a stage well beyond rational discussion during their tantrums, so there is little point in trying reason with your toddler. But this shouldn't preclude you from talking to your child about the way he is making you feel or describing how you imagine he must be feeling.

Even if your toddler is too hysterical to take in the actual meaning of your words, the tone of your voice and the realization that you are there will help soothe him. If you can stay calm, yet obviously involved with your child, he should come to realize that even when he is having difficulty coping, he still has your unconditional love. He will also be able to see how adults manage their frustrations and, eventually, he should start to learn from your example.

Express your feelings

One of the advantages of talking to your child in this manner is that it lets you keep in touch with your own feelings, which will help you stay in control of your emotions. This, in turn, will make you much less likely to react in anger and behave in a way that will prove counter-productive in the long term, such as shouting at, or even slapping, your child. Once you've got all these emotions out in the open, you should find that there is little left for you to brood on once your toddler's tantrum is over.

**Life can be very hard when you're only little –
rather than talking *at* your toddler from above,
get down to her level and talk *to* her face to face.**

Talking through your feelings, even if your child isn't listening, will help to give you a clearer understanding of why the tantrum came about. You may be able to identify areas where you could have acted differently or defused the situation. You may gain a better understanding of why your child behaved in a certain way.

Be honest

The important thing during these usually one-sided conversations is to be honest about the way you are feeling. Tell your toddler if you feel furious, exhausted or miserable. Don't blame him for these emotions, but let him know that they affect you and make you less tolerant of his bad behavior. The aim is to let him know exactly what you feel and why you are feeling it, and still leave him with his self-respect intact.

Show that you empathize

It may help to go on to describe how you think he is feeling – that he seems tired, or hungry, for example – and explain that you understand why that makes him cross. Try to show him that you understand how tough and frustrating life can be for a toddler who is unable to do things for himself or find the right words to say what he wants. This will show him that you appreciate his frustrations, and will help him to recognize and find the words for his feelings in the future.

Maintain your composure

Stay calm and talk softly, even if you find it difficult to hear yourself speak over the sound of your toddler's screams. Crouch down and try to make eye contact, but don't get frustrated if your toddler doesn't appear to respond to your voice. Talking softly will show him that you are in control; shouting at your toddler will only encourage him to respond to you in kind. Tempting though it may be to scream back at

him, it will only make the situation worse, so try not to allow yourself to get drawn into the drama. If you do have a screaming match with your toddler you are more likely to end up feeling guilty for having lost control than you are of winning the battle. No one ever really wins in a shouting match, so it's not worth getting involved in the first place.

" SOOTHING RICHIE

My toddler, Richie, used to get into such a rage that I just had to walk away and try to ignore him. But, as soon as the worst was over, he would start sobbing and crying and want me to hold him. I would sit him on my knee and gently rock him while I talked to him about why I thought he had had a tantrum and how it made me feel. It might just have been the sound of my voice, but it seemed to calm him.

"

dealing with breath holding

During a regular tantrum your child has a whole armory of weapons he will use to try to wear you down and get his own way, from kicking and screaming through to biting and scratching. In a breath-holding tantrum your child takes this all a step further and voluntarily holds his breath until he passes out.

This kind of super-tantrum – technically known as cyanotic attack – can be extremely alarming. Fortunately, most toddlers do not indulge in this type of tantrum, but those who do may have anything up to 10 attacks a day. Breath holding most commonly occurs from 18 months to 4 years of age, although it may be seen as early as a year.

What happens?
Usually, your child will give a few long, drawn-out cries and then, on the last one, he will completely empty his lungs. For the next 15

seconds or so he will deliberately hold his breath until he goes blue in the face or passes out. Once unconscious, his body automatically switches over to "automatic pilot" and he will start to breathe again. The whole episode is likely to be over within a minute and does your toddler no harm, although this doesn't make it any less frightening.

How should you react?
Hard as it may be, you need to treat this type of tantrum like any other. If possible, try to distract your child the moment you see him getting ready to hold his breath. If your child continues to hold his breath and passes out, stay calm and watch him carefully until he regains consciousness.

The moment you see him coming round you should try to move away so that when he opens his eyes he doesn't see an audience. This way he won't learn that breath holding gets him more attention. If the attacks persist you should discuss them with your doctor to check that there is no physical problem that needs to be dealt with.

It is important that others around your child, such as family members, carers and friends, treat these attacks in the same way. Once the episode is over, don't discuss it in front of your child. If everyone around him ignores his behavior he will soon learn that breath holding isn't going to have the effect he wants.

> ## " IGNORING ANNA
>
> The first time Anna had a breath-holding tantrum and passed out I was frantic. I rushed her off to the doctor who then explained what had happened. Ignoring them is the hardest thing to do, but we all try to make as little of them as we can. I also make sure I avoid the triggers I know will set her off. "

6 Toddler taming techniques

Toddlers are not born naughty, destructive and argumentative, but they often acquire these traits as they grow and develop. Their natural curiosity and the need to test themselves and others can lead them into all kinds of mischief. Although this stage of a child's development can be hard to live with, there are plenty of steps you can take to help you both get through this often difficult period.

toddler proofing your home

Your toddler is naturally curious so it is quite normal that she will want to touch and feel things – as you will have encouraged her to do with her toys when she was younger. Now that she is more independent she is likely to get herself into all sorts of trouble because it will be your belongings and other household items that have become the objects of her curiosity. If you don't want to spend the next couple of years or so saying "no" to your child – and coping with all the tantrums this will cause – you will need to take steps to toddler proof your home.

The easiest way to do this is to remove items of value so that they are well out of reach, and to keep dangerous objects under lock and key. It is impossible to make your home completely toddler proof, but safety locks, latches and covers will go a long way toward protecting both your toddler and your possessions.

Everyday items

Once you've banished your best possessions and put knives, scissors and other sharp objects under lock and key, you may think that you can relax. However, there are other everyday items that your toddler will be able to create havoc with if she can get her hands on them.

Make-up, felt-tip pens and indelible markers can cause quite a mess, especially if they are applied to walls or furniture. Medicines and some first-aid items can be potentially fatal in your child's hands. Sometimes parents forget about household products such as bleach, drain cleaner and dishwashing detergent, which are often stored within a child's reach under the sink. Garden sheds frequently contain weed

Attach some child-safety locks to your cupboards to stop your pots and pans being spread all over the floor. Your toddler may be a bit put out at first, but stopping bad habits now will save you a lot of tears and tantrums later.

killer and fertilizers, which need to be kept well out of reach of curious little fingers. You can make all of these areas toddler proof and give yourself peace of mind – make sure medicines are kept in a high, preferably locked cupboard, put safety latches on cupboards and a lock on the garden shed.

Prohibited areas

It may be that there are places in your home that you simply can't make toddler proof – perhaps you have a living room with a white carpet or cream furniture, which you don't want spoilt with sticky fingers and upset drinks and food. Or you may have a workshop full of tools that could be dangerous, but it's simply not possible to have them under lock and key all the time.

Your toddler has to know from a very early age that there are areas that are prohibited to her (unless she is with you or another adult). If you introduce these restrictions from the age when your child first starts toddling around on her own, she is more likely to accept them as normal as she becomes older and more independent.

WATCH **POINT...**

There are countless potential choking hazards around the average home. Coins, pen lids – anything of a size that your toddler might put in his mouth should be kept well out of reach.

If your toddler does swallow something and starts to choke, encouraging him to cough may be all that's needed. If this doesn't work, bend him forward and give five sharp thrusts between his shoulder-blades using the heel of your hand. If this fails you may need to try chest thrusts. Kneel behind your toddler and place your fist, thumb inward, against his breastbone. Grasp the fist with your other hand and pull sharply inward and upward. Do this five times at the rate of one every three seconds. If the obstruction still hasn't cleared, or your child appears weak or stops breathing, call for emergency assistance.

CHOKING

Garden rules

Your toddler will enjoy being able to run around in a garden. However, safety here is paramount, especially if the garden has access to a street or a road. Fences need to be secure and gates should be locked shut so that there is no risk of your child escaping when your back is turned. Items of play equipment should be suitable for your toddler's age, so that they are safe for her to use without constant supervision. Make sure that you check them regularly for any broken parts or structural defects. Items such as swings and climbing frames should be placed on a suitable soft surface such as grass, never on concrete.

If there are any areas of the garden that could be a danger to your child, you will need to make them out of bounds by fencing them off. Don't expect your toddler not to go near the garden pond just because you said she couldn't – cover the pond with netting to prevent her falling in and endangering herself.

Playpens

Some parents use playpens to keep their children safe and out of mischief. Others think it is wrong to restrain a child in this way. It's certainly true that children need space to run around and any use of a playpen should be minimal. But it may be an answer for short periods when you both need a break, and can be very useful when you have to answer the door or go to the bathroom. Occasionally parents have been known to sit in the playpen themselves – on a chair with a good book – while their child runs riot around the room!

out and about

Toddlers have no road sense and no real understanding of danger, so they should never be allowed out unless they are under close supervision. Even being closely supervised is sometimes not enough to prevent determined absconders from running off. Young children have a well-developed sense of adventure, which can make them unconcerned about straying from their parents' side.

Everyone has at sometime heard the announcement in the supermarket requesting the parent of a small child to go to the customer help desk to collect his or her offspring. Most parents will have clutched their own child's hand a little more firmly, while giving a small sigh of relief that it was someone else's child that had been lost, not his or her own.

Serial absconders

If your child regularly escapes your clutches in a public place you can take comfort from the fact that this type of behavior is generally short-lived. The novelty of running away from you and having you chase after her should soon lose its appeal. Of course, knowing that doesn't make it any less of a nightmare while your toddler is behaving this way.

There is little point in trying to reason with your toddler, or in explaining the dangers of running off or being separated from you, because she is simply too young to understand what you are saying. To her, it's all part of a game – you running around after her is great fun and therefore hugely attractive.

If your toddler insists on running off at every opportunity, you will have to resort to other measures to keep her safe. Try keeping her strapped in her stroller, or, if this causes too much trouble or isn't practical, you could insist that she wears a harness with reins or a wrist link band with an adjustable length rein. These last two will give your child a degree of freedom while preventing her from actually running away

A wrist link band may give you more peace of mind when you're out and about with your toddler.

from you. Try not to use these restraints too often, though, or she may take longer to learn to take responsibility for herself.

Toddler safari

While you will inevitably have to restrain your child's more adventurous instincts when you are out on the roads or around the shops, you should also provide opportunities for her to explore the outside world at her own pace. Take her to a playground where she can safely run around and explore within the physical confines of the playground's boundaries. Or take her to the park and be ready to run around with her rather than directing her route. Keep her under close supervision but allow her go wherever her impulse dictates.

Seat-belt battles

Children often object quite strongly to being belted into a car seat. Sometimes the trouble doesn't stop with getting them to sit in the seat

> ## " LUCY'S GAME
>
> By the age of four, Lucy had discovered that all she had to do to get attention while we were out shopping was to walk away from me while my mind was elsewhere and tell someone she was lost. Then, as if by magic, she would hear her name being called out over the public address system. Apart from making me panic every time, it was also very embarrassing. In the end, I insisted that she wore a wrist link so that she had to stay close by me. "

while you put the safety harness on – it continues when an older toddler discovers how to unbuckle the safety harness by herself and then tries to get out while you are driving along. By law, your toddler has to be belted into a car seat for her own safety, which means that neither of you have a choice about this, so you will have to be very firm with your toddler if this happens.

No matter how much fuss she makes, you need to explain that if she wants to go out in the car with you she will have to sit in her car seat and wear a seat-belt. The alternative is that she doesn't go with you in the future. If necessary, demonstrate this – perhaps by leaving her behind when she has made a fuss about getting into the car seat or by turning round and going home when she has tried to get out of her seat. She should soon learn that you mean what you say and start to behave in the car.

separation anxiety

Some toddlers insist on hanging onto their parents' hands like limpets and become very distressed if they get separated, even if only for a second. In some cases, something as simple as the parent leaving the room can start the tears flowing. If your child becomes upset at the idea of being parted from you, or kicks up a fuss every time you try to go out of the house without her, she is probably suffering from some degree of separation anxiety. And it can be hard trying to live your life when you have to go through a drama just get out of the door.

Saying goodbye

When you do have to leave your toddler, tell her that you are going, make sure she understands that you'll be back, give her a quick hug and go. Don't drag out the leaving period – it will only give your toddler more time to get worked up.

Don't be too alarmed if she puts on a major show complete with tears, screams and sobs. You can be fairly certain that the tantrum will have stopped by the time you're out of the gate – without an audience to persuade, she'll see little point continuing. If you need any convincing of this, try returning a few minutes later to take a look through the window. Whatever you do, though, don't let your child see you as if she does, she'll have a tantrum every time you go in the hope that it will bring you back again.

The ideal people to look after your child when you go out are those with whom she is very familiar, such as a relative or close friend. If you leave her at someone else's house, make sure that she has her favorite toys and her security blanket or other comforting items with her. Try to spend

Separation anxiety is hard on both of you, but it's something that most toddlers go through to some extent. Try to be upbeat when you say goodbye, as any negative feelings will be picked up on by your child.

a little time with her in her new surroundings so that she has a chance to get acclimatized before you go.

Going to nursery

By the time your child starts at a playgroup or nursery, she should be old enough to cope with being separated from you, but you will need to take things slowly at first. Prepare your child beforehand by telling her what to expect. Explain how you will take her and leave her for a while, but that you'll always be back for her at the end of the session. The first time you take your child, it may be a good idea to spend the first hour with her until she has got used to being with the other children. When you have decided that it's time for you to leave, say goodbye and go, no matter how much fuss your child makes.

If your child doesn't settle within the first few weeks she may well be genuinely unhappy. If this is the case, you need to decide whether it is better leave things for a few months and try again when she is a bit more mature. Of course, this option may not fit in well with your plans, especially if you want to return to work. You may want to consider other childcare options that might suit her better, such as a child minder or leaving her with a relative she already knows well.

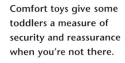

Comfort toys give some toddlers a measure of security and reassurance when you're not there.

unusual behavior

Just like adults, toddlers have their good days and their bad days. Even the sweetest tempered toddler can behave like a little monster when she is feeling out of sorts. If your toddler is being particularly awkward, ask yourself whether she might be hungry, tired or even ill. If any of these factors are at work, you may need to sort them out before you can expect her to behave more reasonably.

Tiredness

Toddlers can become very tired and irritable if they don't get enough sleep. If your child is a bad sleeper and wakes several times a night, she will need more rest during the day than a child who regularly has eight hours uninterrupted sleep a night. Your child may need a short nap in the morning and the afternoon if her nights are very disturbed. Don't let her sleep too long, but allow just enough rest time for her to replenish her energy levels.

Very often, children become tired and fractious long before their accepted bedtime, which is why

There are many reasons why your toddler can become unusually grumpy, and you will need to identify the cause of her upset before you can expect her to behave.

the end of the day can become difficult for both parents and toddlers. Parents are often so attuned to this hyper-alert, overtired state that they miss the more subtle signs that precede it (see box). You could try moving your child's bedtime to coincide with her peak of tiredness, so that you avoid all the tears and upset that occurs when your child is tired. Creating a relaxing bedtime routine, perhaps with a bath, a story and a final hug, will also help.

Hunger

Being hungry can put anyone in a bad mood, and toddlers are certainly no exception. Although you will want to encourage regular mealtimes, there is always room for a healthy snack in your toddler's busy life. Take fruit, sandwiches or

---

WATCH **POINT...**

At the end of the day, look out for early signs of tiredness. These occur when your child is naturally tired, which might not be when your routine says that it's bedtime.

Signs to watch out for include eye rubbing, yawning, general irritability, dragging and loss of interest in toys

TIREDNESS

pieces of cheese with you when you go out, or have them ready when you collect your child from playgroup or nursery. These are much better for her than potato chips, cookies and candies, but offered to her as a snack they will still be thought of as a treat by your toddler. In fact, you may find that you can get your child to eat more food as a snack than you can when she is sitting down to a proper meal.

Avoid being persuaded to go into fast food restaurants when you are out with your toddler. Much of the food on offer is high in fat and has little nutritional value. Some also contains a lot of additives, which can make some children more hyperactive (see page 36). Of course, the occasional burger and chips won't hurt, but don't make them a regular feature of your child's diet.

Illness

If your child is sick she is very likely to be grumpy. After all, adults often feel pretty miserable when they are sick and there is no reason why your child shouldn't, too. If you suspect that your child is behaving badly because she is ill you will need to treat her gently. Start by finding out what is wrong and then decide whether medical treatment is required. If the complaint is minor you can help your toddler by giving her lots of attention and plenty of cuddles. Quiet activities such as reading stories, or doing a puzzle together may be all that is needed to make her feel better.

If the complaint is more serious and your toddler needs to be seen by a doctor, you will have to devote more attention to her. She is likely to be scared and may even refuse to cooperate if the doctor wants to examine her. You will need to be gentle, but firm and very reassuring so that your child understands that anything that is to be done is to make her feel better. As long as she knows that you will be with her, offering your love and support, she is more likely to accept any treatment that has to be given. See the box on page 23 for advice on when you should take your child to see a doctor.

CHILD'S PLAY

Doctors and nurses

Many toddlers find trips to the doctor or the hospital rather overwhelming, especially if they have to stay overnight. You can get your child used to the idea, and make everything seem a little more familiar, by playing doctors and nurses before you go – try asking her to look after a favorite doll or teddy bear. You want your toddler to view the trip as an exciting novelty, not something she should be frightened of.

no-win situations

There may be occasions when you find yourself in a conflict that you cannot possibly win. Either your toddler has outmaneuvered you, or the time and the place isn't right for dealing with the problem. Sometimes, it can be that you are simply too tired to argue any more.

If you end up in this situation, you need to accept it and be prepared to give in gracefully. After all, there is no point in having a head-to-head confrontation with your toddler when you know you have absolutely no chance of winning. Although this type of situation can potentially occur at any time, there are certain occasions when it can prove especially difficult to get an unwilling toddler to budge.

Lack of time

When you are in a hurry there is nothing more exasperating than a child who is deliberately dawdling. But very often the more you try to speed things along, the slower she becomes. Toddlers often behave like this because they want to keep you with them for as long as possible, or, even though they know you will be angry, they want get your attention for a little longer. Sometimes it's just because they don't like having their routine upset.

Accept that there will be times when you just can't win. Try to anticipate these situations and avoid them. Whatever you do, don't let them turn into energy-sapping confrontations.

The situation is fraught with possibilities for tantrums on both sides, so if you can, avoid a head-on conflict. Try picking your child up — unwashed, half-dressed, or without her outdoor clothes — and take her as she is to wherever you are going. At least this way you will still be in control of the situation and your child will have learned that deliberately dawdling doesn't achieve anything.

Feeding

Fighting over food is a waste of time and energy. You can prepare the food, you can put it in front of your toddler, but you can't force her to eat it. If your toddler refuses food, in the end all you can do is take it away without offering anything in its place and comfort yourself with the fact that children don't deliberately starve themselves to death (see pages 30–31 for more advice on dealing with food refusal).

Potty training

Toilet training is fraught with difficulties — if your toddler doesn't want to go, or if she wants to go at an inappropriate time, then no amount of threatening will make her comply with your demands. Toddlers often reach a stage of physical readiness at around the same time that they start to challenge and test their boundaries — the so-called "terrible twos." If you get angry, you may make your toddler even more resentful and unwilling to learn. Alternatively, she may enjoy the power that this type of reaction gives her over your emotions. Exasperating as this may be, you might as well just accept the situation and wait until your toddler reaches a more cooperative phase.

If your toddler starts to wet or dirty herself after a period of being dry, there is even greater need for restraint. This type of regression is commonly associated with some type of stress or

---

Avoiding no-win situations

✔ Set a good example — children copy their parents, so if you lose your temper frequently, refuse to back down, or never admit you are wrong, your child will think this is an acceptable way to behave

✔ Steer clear of situations that you know are likely to provoke a tantrum

✔ Encourage good behavior by using plenty of praise and avoid confrontations over things that you know may lead to a power struggle

✔ Be ready to distract your toddler if you see him becoming frustrated because he is finding something difficult

✔ Offer choices whenever possible, so that your toddler feels that he has some control over his life

✔ If you know you are in the wrong, apologize

✔ When nothing else works, be prepared to give in gracefully

---

illness. If your toddler is ill — diarrhea and urinary tract infections can both result in frequent accidents — then she cannot help herself. If she is reacting to something she finds stressful — such as a change in routine or an upset at home — then confrontation will only exacerbate the situation. Periods of regression are usually only temporary, so be sympathetic and try to accept the situation.

If your toddler doesn't want to go to sleep right away, she may settle quietly in her bed if you give her a book to look at.

Giving in gracefully

Letting your toddler do something you have told her not to do may go against all the rules about being consistent, but sometimes you have to bow to the inevitable. There is no point making yourself feel bad about not living up to your own expectations – in the end, it is better for both of you if you avoid the confrontation.

Don't feel that you always have to get your own way, simply because you are an adult. Letting your toddler win the occasional battle can help her feel that she has more control over her life. This can improve her self-esteem and may encourage her to take more responsibility for her actions.

The key to giving in gracefully is to stay in control – don't allow the situation to escalate and don't begin making empty threats you know you can't enforce. Stay calm and, if you can see that you are not going to make your toddler budge, quickly move the conversation on to another subject or get your toddler to start doing something that you know you can have more control over.

Sleep

Bedtime can be fraught with problems, too. You can get your child bathed and changed for bed, put her into her bed, even keep her in her room, but you cannot make her sleep unless she wants to. Even if your toddler does want to obey you, this is not always enough – as any insomniac knows, trying to force sleep to come can have quite the opposite effect. No matter how much you tell your toddler to shut her eyes and go to sleep, this will not make the slightest difference if she has convinced herself that she can't or simply doesn't want to. It's much better to leave her in her bed, make sure she is comfortable, and wait for nature to take its course.

When to apologize

Every parent gets it wrong at some time – when this happens the best course of action is to admit it and say you are sorry. Perhaps you have been cross with your child because you are feeling stressed and tired, rather than because she has done anything to deserve your wrath. Or you may have used bad language in front of her, even though you have always told her off when she has used "bad" words.

If this happens, it's important to remember that you may be a parent but you are also human, and are therefore allowed to make mistakes. Don't beat yourself up about it – it's how you handle the situation now that matters. Some parents find it hard to apologize to their child because they think it makes them look stupid or weak. But by admitting to your child that you made a mistake and explaining why this happened, not only will she understand the situation better, but also you will help her understand that you, too, have feelings and emotions.

The positives

By apologizing to your child, you will show her that there is no shame in admitting you are wrong or in saying "sorry." This is an important lesson for your toddler. If you want her to learn to be honest and be willing to admit her mistakes, you will need to give her a good example. Showing your toddler that you are not perfect, but that you do try your best, will help her to deal more happily with her own imperfections.

Getting out

Sometimes your child's behavior may simply become too much for you, pushing you right to the limit of your patience. Nothing you do or say makes any difference to the situation, so that you end up wanting to join your toddler on the floor and have a tantrum too. This feeling of having reached the end of your tether usually happens in the confines of your home, because both you and your toddler are likely to be more emotionally restrained in public.

When you feel like this, you need to find yourself some space, away from home, so get up and get both of you out as quickly as you can. Pick up your child and go for a walk, visit the mall, in fact, do anything that takes your mind off your toddler's behavior. She is likely to be so surprised by your sudden change of tack, that she stops whining and turns back into that bright, carefree toddler whose company you so enjoy.

frequently asked questions

? My youngest child has been diagnosed as having special needs. Is it fair for me to expect her to conform to the family rules that my other children have to follow?

Even though it may take much longer for your toddler to understand what she is and isn't allowed to do, it is important that she learns to follow the same rules as your other children. You need to be consistent in your approach and it will make things harder for her, in the long run, if you only expect her to obey the family rules some of the time. With a lot of patience she should eventually learn what is expected of her.

? My four-year-old son simply wrecks his room if I send him there as punishment. I get really angry with him, but it doesn't make any difference. Is there anything else I can do to stop him doing this?

Your best course of action is to appear totally unphased by the chaos he has caused. Make no comment until later, when you tidy up together. Or, try telling him that you are very unhappy about the mess and insist that he tidies it up himself, while you supervise.

? I have just given birth to my second child and my once delightful toddler has turned into a tantrum-throwing monster. Why is he behaving like this and what can I do about it?

Toddlers often revert back to babyish behavior and tantrums when there is a new baby on the scene. Your child probably feels he is missing out on some of your attention and that acting as a baby will help him get it back again. Some children go even further and start wetting themselves or waking at night wanting to be cuddled.

Although there is no quick solution, the best answer may be to allow your toddler to be babyish if that is what he wants, but remain firm about your rules so that he feels safe and secure. Spend time with just the two of you each day, and constantly reassure him that you love him and tell him how special he is. Once he has got used to the new arrival he will soon want to be a big boy again.

? My three-year-old daughter has started telling lies. Is this normal and how should we deal with the problem?

Toddlers often get confused or forget what has happened so that it seems as though they are deliberately lying when they tell an untruth. But, at this age, your daughter won't be lying in the premeditated adult sense of the word. In fact, many toddlers truly believe that by denying that they did something bad the misdeed will simply disappear and they will be able to avoid the consequences of their actions.

Try to deal with your child's lies calmly. Explain the difference between fact and fiction and make allowances for her imagination. Once she old enough to know the difference between telling lies and telling the truth she should also have learned that honesty really is the best policy.

? I keep hearing about the terrible twos, tantrums and what monsters toddlers can be. Are there any good things to say about this stage of a child's development?

Toddlers can be delightful, entertaining and fun loving, and most of the time they think you are the most wonderful person in the world. They can lift your spirits when you are feeling down. If you understand what makes your toddler tick — wanting to be independent one minute, then needing to be your baby the next — you will be more likely to enjoy this stage of your child's development. Keep a positive attitude and concentrate on the fun side of your toddler's life. Your toddler will grow up fast, so make the most of this special time while you can.

index

acknowledgments

Special thanks to my friend Clare and her toddler son George for their help in writing this book. Thanks to my children, Dominic, Lucy, and Kate, without whom I wouldn't have had first-hand experience of toddlerhood. Thanks too, to my husband Robin for giving me the belief that I could reach those seemingly impossible deadlines, and to my editor, Tom Broder, for making it all happen so smoothly.
Alison Mackonochie

The publishers would like to thank:
Production Karol Davies and Nigel Reed
Computer Support Paul Stradling
Picture Research Sandra Schneider
Photography Jules Selmes
Photographer's assistant David Yems

picture credits

1 (top right) photos@imagesprite.com
6 Rolf Bruderer/Corbis 9 Getty Images
15 Getty Images 18 Getty Images
20 Larry Williams/Corbis 25 Getty Images
27 Powerstock 30 photos@imagesprite.com
32 Getty Images 34 Jennie Woodcock;
Reflections Photolibrary/Corbis
36 Elizabeth Hathon/Corbis 45 BabyBjörn
47 Getty Images
52 LWA-Sharie Kennedy/Corbis
54 photos@imagesprite.com
57 Ariel Skelley/Corbis
61 photos@imagesprite.com 62 Getty Images
69 photos@imagesprite.com 72 Getty Images
76 Getty Images
80 photos@imagesprite.com
82 www.thebabycatalogue.com
84 Getty Images
86 photos@imagesprite.com
88 Mother and Baby Picture Library/
Ruth Jenkinson

Front jacket Getty Images